MW00328961

# PALAZZI OF TUSCANY

© 2000 – librimoderni, Udine, Italy

All rights of reproduction, in the whole or in part,
of the text or the illustrations, are reserved
throughout the world.

Project management: Fabiola Beretta
Layout: Gilberto Brun
Editing: Jessica Basso

Original title: Palazzi di Firenze e di Toscana

© 2000 for this English edition:
Könemann Verlagsgesellschaft mbH
Bonner Strasse 126, 50968 Cologne

Translation from Italian: Gerald Binding, David Ginn
and Katron Sutherland in association with Cambridge
Publishing Management
Editing: Frances Brown in association with Cambridge
Publishing Management
Typesetting: Cambridge Publishing Management
Proofreading and Indexing: Lizzie Frege, Cologne
Project Management: Jackie Dobbyne and
Debra Sellman for Cambridge Publishing Management
Project Coordination: Nadja Bremse-Koob
Production: Ursula Schümer
Printing and Binding: Stige

Printed in Italy

ISBN 3-8290-6397-0

10 9 8 7 6 5 4 3 2 1

# PALAZZI OF TUSCANY

Text:
CARLO CRESTI and CLAUDIO RENDINA
Photography:
MASSIMO LISTRI

KÖNEMANN

*Acknowledgement*

We wish to thank all the owners of the buildings, who by their
kindness and co-operation have made it easier to bring this book
to fruition.

Antonio Stella
*Director of Magnus Edizioni*

# CONTENTS

CARLO CRESTI

# THE FROWNING FACE OF THE TUSCAN PALAZZO

# The history and appearance of the domestic fortress in an urban landscape

The private palazzo began to take on its typically urban form once the gloomy and military appearance of the medieval castle, the feudal ruler's residence outside the town walls, was softened by its transference to the city. It was a form noticeably distinct from the turreted and public palazzo-fortress that proudly announced itself as the seat of municipal government.

The new building, which was to develop its characteristics during the 15th century, erected exclusively for the enjoyment of the families of rich merchants and bankers, was no other than a castle with a less war-like look, lacking towers, escarpment walls, and the drawbridge, but with a projecting upper cornice in place of the castellated platform, a viewing gallery instead of a sentry's walk-way, double and triple-mullioned windows instead of loopholes, and a central courtyard surrounded by an arched gallery on columns.

The private urban palazzo, which toned down the aggressive character of the feudal castle, was a suitable expression of the wishes of a buyer whose wealth was recently acquired and who was looking to assert his rank. He wanted to emulate in some way, and especially through the grandeur of his residence, the prestige of the feudal ruler whose aristocratic lineage originated in the granting of lands by king or emperor. From the earlier fortified feudal style, the new palazzo preserved at least the solid masonry of the whole of the first floor, a strong foundation, like a metaphorical rock, formed of and defended by projecting and massive superimposed and rusticated stone blocks; and on this floor too, the windows were placed high above street level and protected by huge iron grills, to guard against possible attacks from hostile political cliques and factions. Moreover, the solid construction of the palazzo, which guaranteed that it would have a long life, was also intended to ensure the continuance of the owner's family line.

With the spread of these private palazzi some aspects of earlier town lay-out changed too; the building of the palazzo of a notable family tended both to take over and merge together small groups of modest houses and to break up properties, often creating an urban "island" of overbearing size. The newly built aristocratic palazzi, large and imposing, changed the face of streets and squares, towered over the dwellings of the people, and led to an increase in size of other buildings. In fact, the domineering character of the old castle, transferred to the town and assigned a role in the less severe appearance of the seigniorial palazzo, survived in the updating and "substitutions" of this new building. This was despite the fact that the palazzo had its own domain, physically and symbolically, its own function as an urban observatory from which to manage property and business affairs in social and environmental surroundings quite other than those outside the town in which the castle of the feudal ruler formerly fought its battles.

The metamorphosis of the fortified castle into the protected patrician palazzo, built against an urban back-drop, gave birth to a special kind of dwelling that, while remaining an outward sign of the self-regard and social ambition of the owner, allowed this vanity to take a form that was not too

*Anonymous 15th-century view of Florence, showing, in addition to the main public buildings, the larger private palazzi.*

The Renunciation of Worldly Goods (*History of Saint Francis*), by Giotto, Cappella Bardi, Church of S. Croce, Florence.

*View of the Palazzo Medici from the Via Larga; by Apollonio Giovanni, detail for the* Aeneid *of Virgil, ms. 492, Virgilii Opera, Biblioteca Riccardiana, Florence.*

*On the following pages, the frontage of the Palazzo Pitti, Florence, original size.*

11

*Palazzo Rucellai, Florence, general view.*

aggressive, however grand and persuasive, and that would not arouse the envy of fellow citizens or affront their traditional Tuscan sense of thrift.

The passage from castle to palazzo is marked by architectural characteristics that were influenced by the aesthetic "temperance" of contemporary Renaissance culture being professed in Florence.

In an early and surprising representation, an urban palazzo, with premonitions of the Renaissance and in a style truly "unknown" in its time, appears for the first time in the fresco *Rinunzia dei beni* (Renunciation of Worldly Goods), painted by Giotto about 1325 in the Cappella Bardi of the church of S. Croce in Florence. This invention of Giotto's, a happy expression of his artistic imagination and decidedly different from the closed and introverted appearance of contemporary medieval fortified houses, seems extraordinarily ahead of its time, innovative and suggestive of a classicizing monumental approach to building that is not to be met with in later urban architecture in Tuscany. In fact, not even in the High Renaissance is it possible to find tangible evidence of a Tuscan building so "sunny" and

*Palazzo Rucellai, Florence,
detail of the wall base.*

"airy." On a base dado covered with stone, the palazzo planned and represented by Giotto opens up on the second floor, with the arches of three galleries (trabeated and cadenced with slender columns) arranged around what is presumably a courtyard. Thus the galleries, well-lit links between the exterior and the interior, are the openings, the channels of communication, through which the building takes part in the life that surrounds it, and by which the activities of the courtyard are filtered and projected outwards to the adjacent urban buildings, which, though not shown, can easily be imagined.

We can compare the date of the building created by Giotto's imagination with that of the Florentine palazzo built from 1444 onwards by Cosimo de' Medici (the Elder) and designed by Michelozzo, which everyone agrees is the archetypal Renaissance palazzo. We cannot fail to notice that the closed and unrelenting monobloc of the armored Medicean residence on what is now the Via Larga – a parallelepiped on three floors above ground, fortified with ashlar that becomes considerably less thick towards the cornice – is, with its expression of unrelenting suspicion of the outside world, a type of building considerably less emancipated from medieval style, and unquestionably less friendly in its attitude towards the city (and therefore less "modern"), than that conceived by Giotto. Nor does the appearance of the facades of the palazzi built in Florence by Luca Pitti and Filippo Strozzi seem favorable to amicable relationships with the world outside. In the case of the Palazzo Pitti (its design attributed to Brunelleschi and building to Luca Fancelli), the seven large arcades of the second and third floors of the original nucleus of the building, arranged as a frieze to an uninterrupted balcony (an absolutely exceptional element in the architecture of the Tuscan palazzi of the period), might lead one to believe that there had been some increase in confidence that marauding citizens could be deterred. However, it is more likely that the size of the arcades framing the windows can be accounted for either by the location of the palazzo almost on the edge of the city, backing

The front of the Palazzo Rucellai may seem different, more "attractive" and gracious in effect, because of the tissue of "classical" reminiscence created by the imposition of three orders of pilaster strips. These rise from the reticulated back of the *panca di via*, or stone bench, are interrupted horizontally by continuous trabeation, and finish at the cornice, because the upper loggia lies behind the plane of the facade. However, the vertical members, which scarcely stand proud of the facade, are only non-load-bearing ornament, decoration stamped in relief on the facade and having no structural function; the imposition of "classical" reminiscence is rather puzzling, because the size of the ashlar blocks of the facade does not seem to correspond to the horizontal and vertical division of the stones that form the various courses (including those that make up the pilaster strips); the present appearance of the stones seems to be a later addition, possibly achieved by incising the blocks

*Giuliano da San Gallo, wood model for the Palazzo Strozzi, Florence, detail of a facade, Museum of the Palazzo Strozzi, Florence.*

on to the walls and facing a rising piazza, or by the fact that, standing in isolation, it could make use of a fairly large surrounding open space, which, in addition to giving it wide panoramic views, made it less vulnerable to surprise attacks and discouraged ambushes. Nevertheless, even though "the fenestration was of such size and magnificence," the palazzo of Luca Pitti, the largest ever built in Italy, 35 meters high and 55 meters long, did not forgo the ashlar blocks that, massive and projecting, made it look like a huge stone quarry at the foot of the Boboli hill.

when they were already in place, as these blocks were larger than the incised stones. All this is to say that behind the elegant and attractive surface there is strongly present the idea of a building externally fortified.

The facade of each palazzo, the most evident and telling surface, in that it indicated the differentiation between the public and the private and translated into stonework the ideology of riches and power, was a matter exclusively of the owner's choice. It depended on what way and to what extent he wished to reveal himself to the

*Palazzo Strozzi, Florence, view of the facade on the corner of Via and Piazza Strozzi.*

public; on whether he wanted to annoy or placate his fellow citizens; on how, through the shape and size of his palazzo, he could validate his financial authority and cultural prestige.

Although the palazzo was his most important status symbol, the Florentine and Tuscan owner, nevertheless, was traditionally inclined to think of the city as hostile and his own dwelling as in need of defense; this defensiveness was also expressed in avoiding counter-productive exhibitionism, thereby respecting traditional notions of thrift and, as Vasari wrote, "escaping envy." On this subject

the humanist Leonardo Bruni wrote, in his *Laudatio Florentinae Urbis* (1403), that the behavior of the Florentine was "highly prudent," that it was instinctive in him "not to do anything for show or ostentation, or to pursue a dangerous or useless course, but to act with a steady and calm decorum." Thus it was considered a good rule not to let others learn, from the external magnificence of the palazzo, just how rich you were.

In Florence, at least, and in other urban centers of Tuscany, the palazzo of the important citizen, while expressive in architectural terms of

*Opposite, detail of* The
Coronation of Enea
Piccolomini, *by Bernardino di
Betto, known as Pinturicchio,
Libreria Piccolomini, the
Cathedral, Siena.*

Renaissance individualism, never became a building that was extrovert, transparent, inviting, or attractive in external appearance; it was always severe and sullen, concerned to protect itself from expected and unavoidable threats, rather than committing itself to the hazards of amiability.

It is significant that Cosimo de' Medici the Elder, who understood the psychology of the Florentines and was a master of "political" prudence, judged the princely residence designed by Brunelleschi for the piazza opposite the church of S. Lorenzo "too sumptuous a building," and, so as not to provoke the envy of his fellow citizens, decided not to have Brunelleschi's "very fine, large model" built.

However, Filippo Strozzi, returning from the exile imposed on him by the Medici and determined to compete with the family that was so hostile to him, thought it fitting to have built a palazzo that would look like a challenge. It swallowed up more than 15 pre-existing houses, was an unadorned, powerful cube with a shell of rusticated ashlar, much larger than the Medici residence on the Via Larga, and above all, standing in haughty isolation, was seen by his political opponents as an impregnable mountain of stone. The Strozzi building was described by Ercole I d'Este as "more magnificent than that of Lorenzo [de' Medici]," and Lorenzo Strozzi, Filippo's son, wrote, "if magnificence is recognized and demonstrated… especially in the construction of public and private buildings, it can be said that Filippo not only worked magnificently, but outdid the magnificence of any other Florentine."

That the taking shape of the Palazzo Strozzi, clearly built as a competitive challenge, was an important event for the city is shown by the detailed notes about its construction (from the digging of the foundations in 1489 to its completion in 1504) that the Florentine surveyor Luca Landucci diligently entered in his diary.

By 1504, when the Palazzo Strozzi was finished, the architecture of such a building, despite the impressiveness of its massive structure, was anachronistic, because stylistically it was out of date. Paradoxically, it could be said that, even though the Arnolfini tower of the Palazzo Vecchio rose higher, the Palazzo Strozzi did not differ significantly in its appearance from the solid Palazzo Comunale of Florence. To register fully the monotony of the rigid parallelepiped form of the Palazzo Strozzi, we only have to compare it with the stylistic novelty and tellingly modern use of space proposed by Pinturicchio in 1502 in the representation of the palazzo he conceived and painted as the background of the *Incoronazione di Enea Piccolomini* (Coronation of Enea Piccolomini), in the Biblioteca Piccolomini of the cathedral of Siena. Raised on columns and arches, the building

imagined by Pinturicchio has a fully porticoed first floor, and the living rooms are arranged on the second floor on either side of a gallery in perspective that passes through the whole thickness of the building and that, with two balustraded terraces, underlines the dynamic relationship between the imagined palazzo and its surroundings. Once again, the architecture represented in paintings, with its innovative solutions, outstrips the architecture that was actually being built at the time.

The Palazzo Strozzi, in fact, reproduces almost identically the distinctive characteristics of Michelozzo's Palazzo Medici. These characteristics – monochrome coloring, the compact block with an inner courtyard, the horizontal lines of the cornices marking off the floors, the regular cadence of the windows (twin-mullioned with rounded arches and radiating stones around the arches), coping in the form of a protruding cornice – were imitated and repeated, with some variations in the ashlar facing and the coping (a roof instead of the cornice), in Florentine palazzi belonging to the Strozzin, the Pazzi (c. 1469), the Antinori (1469), and the Gondo (c. 1457), and in Sienese palazzi of the Papesse (which Caterina Piccolomini, sister of Pope Pius II, had built in 1460), the Piccolomini (1469), with the exterior in travertine recalling the appearance of the Florentine Palazzo Rucellai, and the Spannocchi, with its tufa wall surfaces (1473), to which was added in 1879 the facade overlooking the Piazza Salimbeni. Much freer in its forms, and reminiscent of the Gothic in its first order, is the ornate facade of the small palazzo of the Fraternita di Santa Maria della Misericordia in Arezzo (today the location of the Judicial Offices), completed by Bernardo Rossellino in 1435.

The exterior forms of the Palazzo Rucellai in Florence were repeated without any innovations by Bernardo Rossellino in the Palazzo Piccolomini built in Pienza for Pius II (1459–63). The building, with a facing of tufa ashlar, competes in its upper part with the travertine facade of the Cathedral that stands next to it, and is most successful at the rear, which has a three-story loggia that overlooks the hanging garden and a panoramic view of the Val d'Orcia.

In Florence, civic and municipal pride in the number and quality of the private palazzi, both built and under construction, which "redounded to the honor of the city," is witnessed in such works as the *Istoria di Firenze* (History of Florence) between 1380 and 1405, written by Goro Dati in 1409 ("I cannot tell you the great number of citizens' palazzi; the world has no royal palaces that surpass them"), or the *Cronaca fiorentina* (Florentine Chronicle, between 1430 and 1480) of Benedetto Dei, and in the 16th-century *Storia fiorentina* (Florentine History) by Benedetto Varchi. Vasari also recalls "the most amazing

buildings constructed of stone blocks." Even the illustrations to Virgil's *Aeneid*, done by Apollonio di Giovanni c. 1460, show the construction stages of the palazzo of the Medici, which is represented as the royal palaces of both Priam and Dido; and in the "Iconographic Plan of Florence," drawn by Pino del Massaio (1472), and the so-called *Veduta della Catena* (c. 1471–82), some large palazzi (Pitti, Spini, Gianfigliazzi, Medici, Ricasoli, Tornabuoni) are marked as clearly as the larger public and religious buildings.

Savonarola was alone in rebuking, in a sermon preached in 1496 as part of his fearful campaign for repentance, those who lived in "fine houses," accusing them of trying to create "a paradise" in this world, and warning: "You who live in fine houses, decorated with so much gold and so many objects, are in league with the wickedness of men, or of the devil, or perhaps of both."

We should notice, however, that the passion for "raising walls," that is, for the building of a spacious and expensive palazzo, was a luxury investment with no financial return, and not the sign of a flourishing and expanding city economy; rather, the building of the palazzi, which was the biggest building boom in any European city of the period, and the trend towards

*Courtyard of the Palazzo Medici, Florence.*

investing previously accumulated riches in property (newly built and for exclusive personal use), show that it was difficult to diversify by investing business and banking profits usefully within the city or outside.

Benedetto Dei noted that "*Florentia bella* in the time of Cosimo de' Medici and Luca Pitti and Neri di Gino Capponi and Giannozzo Manetti constructed 33 large stone buildings of great renown and at great cost for their own pleasure and honor and that of the people of Florence"; and he goes on to give a list, mentioning "the famous building erected as a house for the Medici," and houses for the Martelli, the Salviati, and the Spinelli, as well as "the great Tornabuoni house," "the great house of the Gianfigliazzi," and the "great house of the Rucellai and that of the Lenzi."

When the small-scale "royal palace" of the merchant or the banker was the family home from which commercial or exchange business was carried out, the palazzo had a first-floor loggia so that the area specifically reserved for dealing would be visible and recognizable from the street. In Dei's annotated memoirs, *Memorie notato* (1470), there is mention of the loggias belonging to the most important families, such as those of "the great house of the triumphant Medici," "the most mighty house of the Pitti," "the rich and mighty house of the Rucellai," "the worthy and rich house of the Pazzi."

For their "exchange bank," the very rich Medici had a double-arched loggia set up at the corner of the palazzo on the Via Larga (a loggia that was closed up in 1517 by the wall required for the superb corbelled windows designed by Michelangelo). In a general way, the loggia opening on to the street functioned as a "shop window" for the display, advertisement, and selling of the commodities, and the greater comfort of the clients; but it was also used for the public celebrations of "rites of passage" of the notable family, such as engagements, marriages, and funerals.

Giovanni Rucellai, to outdo the Medici, and declaring that he was building his loggia "for the honor of our family, to be used for celebrations and sad occasions," had it built (to a model by Antonio del Migliorano Guidotti, according to an anonymous Cadiz writer) in the narrow area of a small triangular piazza, in order to emphasize its dependence on the palazzo he owned.

Benedetto Varchi, revising notes supplied by Dei, agrees that "families that had a loggia were nobler than the others," and is surprised that Dei had forgotten "some that are still standing, and in very public places, too."

In contrast to the fairly uncommon loggia at the foot of or near the palazzo, giving directly on to the street, is the almost continuous first-floor loggia running around the internal courtyard. Almost all the major Florentine residences have this hidden, circumscribed and restful "personal" piazza, a quiet secular cloister around which the life of the palazzo centered and where the family could enjoy its privacy. The walls of this central, rectangular space, cut off from the urban surroundings and hidden from outsiders, could be articulated in the elegant columns and the graceful arcades of the shaded porticoes (which opened up the narrow space to the sky), with twin-mullioned windows or open galleries running along them; all created a calm and welcoming atmosphere that unquestionably contrasted with the unsociable effect of the aggressive, rusticated stone facade overlooking the street.

Varchi, again using Dei, wrote that "between the years 1450 and 1478, 30 palazzi were built in Florence," and in order "not to detract from the posthumous fame of those generous spirits that built them," he gives their names: "Pitti, Medici, Martelli, Gianfigliazzi, Tornabuoni, Rucellai, Pazzi, Pucci, Giuntini, Guardi, Lenzi, Boni, Neroni, Spinelli, Berucci, Strozzi, Ridolfi, Capponi, Salviati, Cavigiani, Gherardi, Neretti, Aldobrandini, Morelli, Antinori, Borromei, Miniati, Albizzi, Niccolini, and Vettori." Beyond the 35 "most worthy ancient palazzi," and the "Palazzo Pubblico of the Signoria and the Podestà," Varchi does not take into account "either the residences of the 21 guilds, which are all large and honorable buildings, or the magnificent edifice of Orsanmichele."

The appearance of the Orsanmichele deserves comment. It is a "palazzo in the form of a fortress for the storage of grain and fodder," built on the route between the seats of political and religious power, unusual both for its function, and for its elevation of pillars that support the cross-vaulting and form a loggia on the first floor (closed in 1380). These carry the parallelepiped of the granary, which is incomparable in the architectural refinement of its outside walls. This granary is, then, a different sort of palazzo, the exterior of which is testimony to the satisfaction the Florentines felt in their knowledge of building and their ability to make a work of art out of a very practical need. The same is true of the proud ostentation of the 14 painstakingly worked marble niches on the outside of the perimeter columns. These house the statues of the patron saints of the ancient guilds, the *Arti Maggiori*, in an unsurpassed exhibition of Renaissance Florentine sculpture.

If the private palazzo of the eminent merchant or banker had the appearance of a less war-like and threatening castle, the Palazzo Pubblico, a symbol of civic values, a center of municipal political power and administration, and the residence of the governor during the Commune, the Republic, the Signoria, and the Grand Duchy, was in effect an urban fortress with a few domestic touches.

Its Salone, where the local magistrates sat and ambassadors were received, was a room for great public occasions, similar to the main piazza, and the churchyard and central nave of the Cathedral. Moreover, it was in the shelter of the Palazzo Pubblico of Florence that the priors of the guilds and the gonfalonier of justice lived "to carry out their functions" for the brief period of electoral mandate provided for by the Ordinances. They were almost recluses and slept in a communal bed chamber divided by wooden partitions. We must remember that in the so-called Palazzo Vecchio, the building of which started in 1299 to house the priors of Florence, gonfalonier, and the magistrates of the Republic, and to protect them from "the threats of the powerful" (that is, city notables excluded from government of the city), the assembly room was the place where the solemn rituals of a "democracy" were enacted. This democracy was something of a fiction, because – as Bernardo Segni noted – "no common people who lived in the city" had access to the administration, "but only notables and those in

*Orsanmichele, Florence, general view.*

21

public office." Given the fact that government was primarily the expression of the political will of the upper middle classes, the word "popular" is an exaggeration.

Again, in Siena in 1298, the decision to build the Palazzo Pubblico (which was completed in 1310) was a consequence of the need for secure accommodation, safe from external interference, for the Nine, the governing magistrates, who represented the interests of the banking and mercantile oligarchy. The intention was to avoid their having to sit, as they had until then, in the houses of city notables – hospitality that could lead to a possible dependency from which they wished to free themselves.

Municipal palazzi were completed in Volterra in 1257, Pistoia in 1294, and Lucca in 1320 (near the church of S. Michele in Foro), not only to improve the appearance of the city, but to act as the obligatory residence, during their period of service, of the "elders" who made up the magistrature. Later, in some cities, these elders were called "priors," over whom the gonfalonier of justice presided.

The functions of the Tuscan public palazzo explain, therefore, the preoccupation with security, and the predominantly enclosed and protected character of the building, intended to discourage any attacks on the institutions of government. Although the Palazzo dei Priori in Volterra is notable for its vertical, severe, and box-like walls, with no openings, surmounted asymmetrically by the tower, and covered with rough, gray sandstone, the equally stony Palazzo Comunale of Pistoia, located next to the Cathedral, seems at least to speak to the adjacent piazza through the continuous portico on the first floor of the facade. In Siena, moreover, the three segments that make up the front of the Palazzo Pubblico (two oblique wings converging on the central component) not only provide a backcloth for all lines of vision from the Campo, but appear, metaphorically, to be embracing the city. It is an open embrace (altogether there are ten entrances to the palazzo), made welcoming by the warm-colored brickwork, the Montagnola limestone at the base, and the travertine of the upper part of the off-centered tower. Surprisingly light in effect, the Torre del Mangia, which was started in 1325, is a very carefully judged counterpoint to the horizontal lines of the palace (the three-windowed top floor and crenellations on both the wings were added in the 17th century). The "amiable" characteristics and undoubted lightness of the architecture of the Palazzo Pubblico of Siena might suggest that its appearance is the consequence of the stable political situation brought about in the early decades of the 14th century by the long rule of the Nine. That is, the differences of character between medieval Tuscan palazzi, both civic and private, could be related to an increase or

*Opposite,* Four Crowned Saints, *Nanni di Banco, the Stone and Wood Workers' Guild Niche by Orsanmichele.*

Doubting Thomas *Andrea del Verrocchio, the Merchants' Guild Niche (carried out by Michelozzo and Donatello) by Orsanmichele.*

*Palazzo Guinigi, Lucca.*

decrease in the quarreling between the cliques and factions within the different cities. In Siena the Palazzi Marescotti (later Chigi Saracini), Sansedoni, and Buonsignori, with their exterior brickwork and graceful orders of triple-mullioned windows, looking domestic rather than defensive, could be a sign that there was a lessening of disturbance and danger from in-fighting citizenry.

The special character of Siena is documented in the *Constituto* of 1297, which, uniquely in the history of medieval towns, provides that the windows of new houses on the Campo shall have "colonnelli," or small columns of stone or marble, presumably to unify the elegant architectural backcloth to the great public piazza that in 1349 was paved with brick.

There is no doubt that the use of brick as a building material, softer than stone, easy to work,

*Palazzo dei Priori, Volterra.*

warm in color, and with a decorative potential, made for the variety, or rather the stylistic individuality, of Sienese architecture, and in very significant ways.

The same can be seen in Lucca, another city with a great and distinctive civic architecture, in which there was at the same period a widespread and typical use of brick, and where the bringing together of brickwork elements produced, even more so than in Siena, original and pleasing decorative effects in the cornices between stories, in window-sills, and in the lintels of window and door arches. These ornamental elements, together with open arcades on the first floor, with twin, triple, quadruple and quintuple-mullioned windows opening into the upper stories, juxtaposed and surmounted so as to almost create loggias, served to lighten the solidity of the walls and give the buildings of the gentle bourgeoisie of Lucca an appearance that was anything but defensive. Typical examples of this are the late 14th-century Palazzo Ottolini Balbani, in the Via Sant'Andrea, and two buildings contemporary with it constructed by the Guinigi, one next to the attractive tower topped with oak foliage, the other opposite it.

Further confirmation of the uniqueness of Siena is found in the richness of pictorial decoration, both secular and religious, that aims to increase the significance of the Palazzo Pubblico by recording in memorial form the important events in the civic history of Siena and by devotional images that witness to the deeply religious nature of the Sienese. In the Cappella dei Nove (Chapel of the Nine), on the first floor of the palazzo, there are frescoes by Simone Martini (1321) and Lippo Memmi (1326). Here,

Vecchietta (c. 1435) painted the *Madonna della Misericordia* (Our Lady of Mercy) surrounded by angels and saints. In the Council Chamber on the *piano nobile* (principal floor), Simone Martini painted, under a light canopy, the great *Maestà* (Madonna in Majesty), illuminated with gold (1315–21), and the *Guidoriccio da Fogliano* (1330–31) as a knight, represented as a haughty and solitary automaton. In the same room Ambrogio Lorenzetti painted the *Mappamondo* (Map of the World, 1344–45), and there is a fresco by Lippo Vanni of *La Battaglia di Val di Chiana* (The Battle of Chiana Valley, 1363). On the three walls of the Sala delle Balestre or della Pace (the Peace or Ballot Room) Lorenzetti stylishly wrote with colors the marvelous allegorical accounts of *Buon Governo* and *Cattivo Governo* (Allegory of Good and Bad Government, 1338). In the Sala Nova (the New Room), later known as the Magistrates' Room, Martino de Bartolomeo decorated the ceiling with the allegorical figures of *Virtù* (the Virtues, 1407), and Spinello Aretino recounted on the walls the *Storie*, or events in the life, of the Sienese pope, Alessandro III Bandinelli Paparoni (c. 1408).

It is worth noting that, in an area influenced by Sienese culture, another municipal palazzo, that of San Gimignano (completed in 1288), has rooms that are adorned by a notable series of frescoes. These frescos are known as: the *Madonna in trona* (Madonna Enthroned, 1317), signed by Lippo Memmi, intended to enhance, through its patron saint, the importance of the council chamber; the *Amore coniugale* (Married Love, 1311), painted by Memmo di Filippuccio in the room of the Podestà; and finally in the courtyard, the *Sant'Ivo che rende giustizia* (Saint

*Palazzo Sansedoni in the background of a view of the Piazza del Campo, Siena.*

The Lily Room, *(Sala dei Gigli), Palazzo Vecchio, Florence; note the coffered wood ceiling, the gold frieze showing the* Marzocchi *supporting the coat of arms of the Commune, the people and the Guelph party. On the walls, the frescoes by Domenico Ghirlandaio.*

Ivo Dispensing Justice, 1507), the work of the skillful artist Sodoma.

In Florence, however, except for the episodic frescoes carried out about 1345 in the chapel of the 13th-century Palazzo del Podestà (later called the Bargello), showing *Paradiso* (Paradise), the *Inferno* (Hell), and *Storie* (stories) of St. Mary of Egypt, Mary Magdalene, and John the Baptist, we do not find any internal decoration of public buildings until the last 30 years of the 15th century, when some murals and distinguished work in wood appear as part of the decoration of the rooms and reception halls of the restructured Palazzo Vecchio. From 1470 onwards impressive coffered ceilings, inlaid and painted, were added to the *Sala de' Dugento* (the Room of the Two Hundred) and the adjacent *Sala degli Otto* (Room of the Eight) on the first floor, as well as the *Sala dei Gigli* (the Lily Room) and the *Sala della Udenzia* (the Audience Chamber) on the upper floor. In the *Sala degli Gigli*, in the cornices of three arches on the same wall, Domenico Ghirlandaio (1482–85) painted frescoes showing *San Zanobi* enthroned and giving a blessing, two *Marzocchi* (Florentine lions) with the arms of the people and the city of Florence, and "heroic" figures of six Ancient Romans, symbols and models of republican liberty (Brutus, Mucius Scaevola, Furius Camillus, Decius Murae, Scipio Africanus, Cicero).

Accustomed to being always on the defensive, and thus used to living in a domestic environment that had hardly any communication with the outside world, the Florentines naturally wanted some relaxation for themselves, some agreeable "liberty" in the furnishing and decoration of their interiors. Although we have to stress that the external decoration of the palazzo, like its austere facade, was very limited (the stone bench, the entrance gate with its studded doors, the wrought-iron lantern – to be seen at the corners of the Palazzi Medici and Strozzi – the banner holders, the torch holders, the ringed hinges, again in wrought-iron, the family coat of arms), we must nevertheless note that the fixed furnishings of the interior of the nobleman's house could boast a wider, more varied, and more refined range of artifacts and effects.

We only have to recall the wall decorations with garlands, coats of arms, intricate floral designs, trefoil arches, and ornamental backgrounds of nature (hedges, trees, fruit, and birds), or the false tapestries, with dark and net curtains, found during the 19th-century demolition of the historic center of Florence in the houses of the Sassetti, the Vecchietti, the Teri, the Catellini da Castiglione, and the Pescioni, as well as in the guild houses and other medieval buildings caught up in the destructive "clearance" of the *Mercato Vecchio* (Old Market) area; or the late 14th-century paintings of horsemen (*Storia della Castellana di Vergi*, History

27

A torch-holder in wrought iron by Niccolò Grosso, known as Caparra, Palazzo Strozzi, Florence.

of the Castellana di Vergi) on the walls of a room in the Palazzo Davanzati, and the legendary *Cavalcata dei Magi*, or Ride of the Three Wise Men (1459–63), a fresco by Benozzo Gozzoli in the chapel of the Palazzo Medici in the Via Larga.

We could mention also the three famous *Battaglie*, or Battles, by Paolo Uccello in the "great ground-floor chamber" of Lorenzo the Magnificent in the Palazzo Medici, the wood and inlaid paneling that surrounds and lines the walls of so many courtly rooms, and the painted panels, often used as bed-heads. The best-known of these are the *Festa danzante*, or Dance (also called *Nozze Adimari*, the Adimari Wedding), by Scheggia, and other secular *Storie* (Scenes) by both Botticelli – who, according to Vasari, "places around a room many paintings surrounded by decorations in walnut, acting as paneling, with many lively and beautiful figures" – and Piero di Cosimo, who, again in the words of Vasari, "painted… in the house of Francesco del Pugliese a room with many incidents showing small figures," and, in the Vespucci house in the Via de' Servi, "scenes of Bacchanalian revelry around the room, in which appear strange fauns, satyrs, and woodland figures, putti and Bacchante, which it is a marvel to see…"

The quality and elegant attractiveness of 15th-century Florentine internal decoration is summed up in the two rooms of an aristocratic house that appear in the frescoes of the *Nascita del Battista* (Birth of John the Baptist) and the *Nascita della Vergine* (Birth of the Virgin) painted in the Capella Maggiore of the church of S. Maria Novella by Domenico Ghirlandaio (1486–90).

Especially in the *Nascita della Vergine*, the richness and the feeling of surrounding comfort seem to stem from the integration of horizontal and vertical architectural elements, articulated by such incident as the Corinthian columns ornamented with candelabra that subdivide the space, and by the wood coffered ceiling that has two large sunken panels surrounded by a fascia decorated with garlands and cherubs' heads. The same organization of horizontal and vertical compositional motifs is found in the wooden panel on the wall of the bed area, with door paneling inlaid with grotesques, and divided by Corinthian columns with carved capitals that support a cornice trabeation, above which are two bas-reliefs of frolicking putti.

We can assume that all the decoration and furnishing represented by Ghirlandaio are based on a room in the palazzo of the Tornabuoni family, who, in 1485, commissioned the great cycle of frescoes for the choir of S. Maria Novella.

Seeing that Filippo Brunelleschi's plan for the Medici palazzo was, distressingly for him, turned down, and that there are serious doubts about his involvement in the design of the Palazzo Pitti, and

Decorations in the "Parrot Room," Palazzo Davanzati, Florence.

given that Michelangelo was not highly esteemed by bourgeois private patrons, we can only conclude that the two greatest Florentine architects were not, as builders of domestic dwellings, especially lucky on their home ground.

Moreover Brunelleschi died in 1446, and it was not until 1517 that Michelangelo, when he returned to Florence, designed, on the orders of the Medici pope Leo X, the corbelled windows that closed in the corner loggia of the Palazzo Medici.

During this period, from 1446 to 1517, anyone who wished to "raise" a family palazzo, or any other building, had to make use of local craftsmen, such as Giuliano and Benedetto de Maiano, or lesser designers, such as Simone del Pollaiolo, known as il Cronaca, and Baccio d'Agnola, who were more compliant with their clients' wishes.

Even Lorenzo the Magnificent employed a second-rate architect, Giuliano da San Gallo, for the design of the Villa Poggio a Caiano (1485) and the proposed new Medici palazzo (1491) that was to be built (to judge from an unclear plan) near the church of SS. Annunziata. Not even the arrival of the great Leonardo da Vinci, author, in about 1515, of a generalized proposal for another Medici palazzo, intended perhaps as the residence of the then governor, Lorenzo di Piero de'

Medici, was to have any effect on the contemporary mediocrity of Florentine architecture, because the proposal was immediately dropped and never even reached the stage of being a plan.

We have only to note the starting and completion dates of the Palazzi Antinori (1461–69), Pazzi (1458–69), Scala (1473), Strozzi (1489–1504), Gondi (1490–98), and Dei (1503–6), to realize that these buildings, in addition to being proof of the low quality of Florentine architecture in the late 15th and early 16th centuries, are influenced by the self-mortifying message spread by Savonarola between 1492 and 1498.

The Palazzo Dei (later called Palazzo Guadagni), despite its original geometric designs (now disappeared) and the top-floor loggia, seems, with its rather stark appearance, to be a compromise between the qualified need to be representative and rigorous penitentialism, or even the product of a transition stage between the facade of ashlar stone and that which is simply plastered, between ostentation and unpretentiousness, leaving it to doors and windows, as ever, to imbue the outside of the building with some style.

In other words, the front wall of the Palazzo Guadagni reminds one of the severity of all those palazzi built before 1520 and referred to in the *Memoriale* (Memoirs) of Francesco Baldovinetti,

*Birth of the Virgin, by Domenico Ghirlandaio, fresco in the Capella Maggiore of the Church of S. Maria Novella, Florence.*

*Facade of the Palazzo Bartolini-Salimbeni, Florence.*

*Palazzo Guadagni, Florence.*

the characteristics of which are chosen from among a number of invariable elements: the "stone bench" as a continuous stylobate, stone facing only on the first floor, corbelled windows, quoins for the whole height of the facade, family coats of arms placed in the center of the facade or at the corners, door and window cornices surmounted by plasterwork, and a protruding roof that replaces the cornice.

Baldovinetti, in *Memoriale*, lists the Palazzi Sforza Almeni in the Via de' Servi, Rosselli del Turco in the Borgo Santi Apostoli, Ginori in the street of the same name, and "many fine houses" in the Via Maggio, these probably being the colorless Palazzi Ridolfi (later called Ricasoli-Firidolfi), Michelozzi, and Zanchini.

To these buildings we can add, as being similar in form, the Palazzo Taddei in the Via Ginori, Florence, the Palazzo Grifoni which was built later in San Miniato al Tedesco (with external facing in brick), the Palazzo Rospigliosi in Pistoia, and the Palazzi Balduini and Pancrazi in Barga (the latter having "diamond-point" door and window cornices). Somewhat similar, and not very exciting, is the facade of the Palazzo Pandolfini (1516–32) on the Via San Gallo, Florence, the asymmetrical side wing of which, covered with a terrace, makes it unlikely that the usual attribution of the plan to Raphael is correct. Even the later (1580) and carefully judged facade of the Palazzo Giacomini (later called Palazzo Larderel), designed by Giovanni Antonio Dosio, is hardly an example of enchanting modeling.

There are, however, some exceptions to the usual canon of forms: the Palazzo Mancini in Cortona (1533) has a facade consisting of a superimposition of orders (stone pilasters on the first floor, Tuscan pilaster strips on the *piano nobile*, pilasters and pilaster strips on the top floor, which terminates with a loggia); the Palazzo Cocchi (on the Piazza Santa Croce in Florence) is notable for a facade entirely in stone and the purely ornamental imposition of small pilaster strips, as abutments to the blind arches, and larger pilaster strips that appear partly to project beyond the base beneath them. In their Florentine palazzo on the Piazza Santa Trinità (1519–32), the Bartolini-Salimbeni insisted on a facade entirely covered with stone, surmounted by cornices, which allowed for the whim of four arched niches on the second floor and four panels set into the third floor (perhaps intended for statues and to make the facade livelier and more plastic), and introduced to Florence the "crossed" windows of Roman origin.

Roman models also influenced the characteristics of the private palazzi of two centers in southern Tuscany, Monte San Savino and Montepulciano, because of the presence in the area of patron families (the Del Monte, Cervini, and Nobili) that had stronger links with the papal court than with that of the Medici. This is seen in

Monte San Savino in the Palazzo Del Monte (today the town hall), attributed to Antonio da San Gallo the elder, built between 1515 and 1517, and notable for the heaviness of its ashlar first floor and the niched windows (the central one of which has a balcony), framed by the pilaster strips that divide the top floor.

In Montepulciano, we find in the Palazzo Del Monte-Contucci (1517–19), apart from the 17th and 18th-century windows of the top floor, niched windows arranged on the *piano nobile* of a facade that is gently provincial in appearance and encased by quoins that clearly rise out of the ashlar blocks.

The Palazzo Nobili-Tarugi, on the Piazza Grande, squat in appearance, seems, because of the unrelated nature of its dimensions, to be a sympathetic and irreverent parody of how architectural orders should be placed above each other. It has Ionic semi-columns in travertine stone, resting on exaggeratedly high plinths, that, taking in the second floor, function as supports for the short Doric pilaster strips of the third floor and the continuous balustrade that was originally intended to run under the corner loggia. In Montepulciano also, there are traces of Roman influence, mixed with hints of Etruscan archaism, in the ashlar base and the plastic treat-ment of the upper windows of the Palazzo Cocconi (wrongly called Del Pecora), which originally consisted of only two floors above ground, and in the Palazzo Cervini (c. 1555), the U-shaped plan of which is rarely met with in provincial urban architecture.

It is not until the middle of the 16th century that we find any signs of an attempt to escape from the outdated banality of many of the facades of the Florentine palazzi. These attempts were limited to those elements (cornices, corbels, scrolls and other decorative devices) that were consistent with plaster surfaces and able to supplement and bring to life, with touches of fantasy, the monotony of the "doors and windows" formula. It was a long time, therefore, before the repetitive and bare facades began to be populated by figures such as lions' heads, ox-skulls, bearded gargoyles, terrifying monsters, mysterious bats; collections of fabulous apparitions, fantastic and allusive stimuli to the imagination, these creatures formed a disturbing world of monsters to be marveled at, that settled in the curves of the corbels, hid in the tympanum of the pediment, spread around the trabeation friezes, and crept into the curls of scrolls, and into the volutes and foliage of capitals.

*Palazzo Del Monte, Monte San Savino.*

Some architectural historians have considered the fabulous and animistic elements that entered as an artistic embellishment into the unornamented code of Florentine architecture as a sign of the mental disturbance that followed the fall in 1530 of the Florentine Republic, which had been declared in 1527. The fertile and uninhibited figuration, the unorthodox virtuosity, were, according to these historians, synonyms for a moral, artistic and social crisis. The loss of republican liberty created, as it were, "monsters," in an involuntary breaking of the artistic bounds.

This theory is not really credible, and it seems more likely that the undisciplined diversions, the inventive acrobatics of Florentine Mannerism, and the crowded figures of Mannerist architecture, stem from a cultural restlessness, a need to emancipate and reinstate the imagination, to free it from the dogmatism of the single-minded, formal and ideal harmony of "Renaissance Classicism." There was also a need to answer the demand for a new and attractive "style" that would reflect a political and cultural situation radically altered by the rise to power, in 1537, of Duke Cosimo I de' Medici, who by his governance and numerous public works left an indelible mark on Tuscany and gave it its true identity as a state in its own right.

After this date, when power was focused in the figure of Cosimo, the facades of the public and private palazzi of Florence and other Tuscan cities were filled with marble busts of the duke (and of the grand dukes who followed him), placed in full view to indicate the adulation, loyalty, and appreciation of the courtly and "favored" owners of the palazzi, who were delighted with the protection of the Medici "deity"; in addition to their propaganda purpose, there was also a clear admonitory, even intimidatory, intent.

The facades of the Florentine and Tuscan palazzi of the Mannerist period are marked by two typical characteristics: the almost universal corbelled windows (taking as their prototype those of Michelangelo in the Palazzo Medici, which were the reference mark for the large consoles that support the sill, creating a parapet similar to a high prie-dieu), and the remarkable assortment of architectural members peopled with monsters and human figures. These characteristics, however, had no influence on the plan or disposition of the masses of the palazzo, which remained for the whole of the 16th century essentially a box-shaped entity, with no signs of any innovative use of space.

With regard to the appearance of human figures on the facades of buildings, it is worth noting the 15 hermae, known as "the faces," representing famous Florentine personalities and arranged over three floors, which make unusual and more attractive the facade of the Palazzo

Altoviti. These were bought in the middle of the 16th century by Baccio Valori, who placed the diverting marble figures on the building in the company of the stern bust of Cosimo I.

The stone hermae, attributed to Bartolomeo Ammannati, are elegant, 16th century, and unusual for Florence, as are the busts of women crowned with Ionic volutes who keep watch on the corbelled windows of the Palazzo Di Montauto in the Via Ginori, and the grotesque male bodies that form the Atlas corbels supporting the balcony of the Palazzo Guicciardini in the street of the same name that runs parallel to the Arno. Male heads, sculpted in high relief, wink from the keystones of the second floor of the three facades of the court-

*Opposite, view of the Palazzo Nobili-Tarugi on the Piazza Grande, Montepulciano.*

*Tympanum of a corbelled window by Bernardo Buontalenti, Palazzo Nonfinito, Florence.*

yard of the Palazzo Pitti (carved by Bartolomeo Ammannati after 1560), and, on the same floor, from the abutments of the arches of the original loggia that opened into the central facade of the courtyard.

Parallel to the human figures are the animal heads, a highly varied and exuberant "stone bestiary" that covered the external surfaces of the palazzi and contributed to the stylistic liveliness of the architectural elements. The rams' heads engraved on some of the keystones belong to the extended repertoire of stone figures that emerge from the rusticated stonework of the Pitti courtyard, as do the ox-heads, of antique origin, on the architraves of the doors in the loggia.

In the Palazzo Grifoni (1563–75), metopes ornamented with ox-heads make up the frieze that runs along at window-sill height on the second

Top left, details of the gargoyles and grotesques (mostly the work of Buontalenti) that decorate the corbelled window of the Casino Mediceo, Florence.

Center left, the capital of the corner pilaster on the facade of the Palazzo Nonfinito.

Top right, the bas-relief coat of arms on the facade of the Palazzo Capponi delle Rainate.

Bottom right, corbel of a window of the Palazzo di Bianca Cappello.

Bottom left, the family coat of arms from the Palazzo de' Rossi.

34

floor and that rises from an exposed brick surface; a goat (the ducal emblem of Cosimo I de' Medici) sits in the center of the stone tablet that surmounts the door of the same building on to the Via de' Servi, and corbels in the form of rams' heads support the impost cornice of the barrel vault in the vestibule.

Single ox-heads appear in relief on the frieze and the keystone of the main entrance of Ammannati's Palazzo Guinigi in the Via Alfani (1565–77), and rams' heads ornament the jambs of the same door and the pilaster strips that frame the family coat of arms. Ox-heads, with bats coming from their mouths, are entangled in the convex volutes of the corbels of the Palazzo Ramirez de Montalvo in the Borgo degli Albizzi (1562–68).

More metopes with ox-heads provide the decoration for the architrave of the majestic entrance of the Palazzo del Governo in Lucca, begun in 1577 to a design by Ammannati.

From the fantastic combination of a wolf and a bat (created by the talented Buontalenti) derive the hybrid zoomorphs that, placed at the top of the corbels, guard, like immobile sentinels, the windows of the Casino Mediceo in Florence (1574). Strangely feathered bats' muzzles poke out from under the volutes of the pediment and hang from the tympana of four windows on the first floor of the Palazzo Nonfinito in the Via del Proconsolo (1593); another bat, the antithesis of sunlight, hides with wings stretched out in the shade of a corbelled window of the Palazzo Bianca Cappello in the Via Maggio (1567), and yet others were set to fly, during the 17th century, and to display their fascinating unpleasantness on the external parapets of the first-floor windows of the Palazzi Covoni and Bartolommei in the then Via Larga.

In the monster category come the angry and sneering gargoyles, the dragons, and the other stone and marble creatures thought up by architects and artists in their search for something temptingly different.

At the Palazzo Diodati Orsetti in Lucca (1541), devilish dragons appear on the columns and archivolts of the doors giving on to the Via del Loreto and the Via Santa Giustina; in the same city, there are grotesque gargoyles on the upper molding of the second-floor windows of the Palazzo Boccella, in the frieze on the facade of the Palazzo Sanminiatelli Antelminelli (1556), and above the windows of the *piano nobile* of the Palazzo Benvenuti.

The faces of fauns, their cheeks and hair transmuted into curvilinear botanical excrescences, are the main subject used in the decoration of the octagonal pilaster strips of the courtyard of the Palazzo Vecchio in Florence, and, as drawings, punctuate the intricate patterns of the coffered ceiling of the Salone dei Cinquecento (Salon of the Five Hundred).

Similar gargoyles, ludicrous perversions of the human form, are found in the frieze of the second trabeation on the facade of the Palazzo Grifoni, and also on the capitals of the corner pilaster strips of the exterior of Buontalenti's Palazzo Nonfinito, built by the branch of the Strozzi family that supported the Medici.

We find examples of innocently terrifying heads, sharply modeled and with unbelievable faces, on the keystones and cornices of the loggia doors of the Palazzo Pitti; emerging from surmounting shells on the tympana of two first-floor windows of the Palazzo Nonfinito; and, as flourishing extensions, curled around the volutes

*Corbelled window, Palazzo Medici, Florence.*

*Detail of the facade of the Palazzo Valori, known as the Palazzo dei Visacci or 'faces', Florence; the marble hermae represent Donato Acciaiuoli and Marsilio Ficino.*

Lanfreducci, later called "Alla Giornata," built in Pisa to a design by Cosimo Pugliani (1594), and the Palazzo Granucci-Cancellieri built in Pistoia to a design by Jacopo Lafri (1613).

However, the desire to introduce changes into the external appearance of the private building, with the aim of making the facade more varied and attractive, combined with the new requirements of the owner, who was concerned to keep down the cost of such changes and ensure that they were fairly restrained, led to a movement to decorate the facades of family homes with paintings or graffito designs, which were "economical" but beautiful.

The diarist Agostino Lapini noted this movement in Florence in June 1575: "a few days before the feast of St. John the first painted facade was revealed." In fact, during the 15th century, simulated architectural members were already being painted in bichrome on the exteriors of Florentine palazzi, and before 1520 Andrea Feltrini had executed some very elegant graffito work on the facades of the Palazzo

*Herma, with bas-relief portrait of Pier Vettori, on the facade of the Palazzo dei Visacci, Florence.*

*Potal of the Palazzo Diodati Orsetti, Lucca.*

supporting the architraves and parapets of the corbelled windows of the house of Bianca Cappello and the Palazzi Covoni and Bartolomei.

The remarkable number of corbelled windows, and their formal characteristics, made for a change of urban image; Florence ceased to be the city of ashlar blocks and became the city of corbelled windows. If the impressive and sullen roughness of ashlar blocks was a strong physical deterrent that discouraged attacks on the palazzo, the shapes of the corbelled windows, projecting from the surface of the facade – invading public space and hindering the passer-by, who had to move to the center of the street – were essentially a "psychological" deterrent, the only purpose of which was to protect the line that marked out domestic privacy. The "guardian" monsters, placed above all on these windows, with their terrifying grimaces, their allusive characteristics, and even comic appearance (which did not take away from their power as charms), were a suitable reinforcement of the calculated, subliminal message.

In urban centers, where the use of corbelled windows was not widespread, the task of in some way discouraging intrusions into domestic privacy was entrusted to the visible aggressiveness of the forms and thicknesses, almost brutal in their coarseness, of the blocks that made up the cornices, and the keystones and trabeations of doors and windows. We can see this in the case of the Palazzi Guglielmi-Pannelini and Tantucci in Siena (1548), both attributed to Bartolomeo Neroni, known as "il Riccio," the Palazzo

*Opposite, graffito decoration of the facade of the Palazzo di Bianca Cappello, Florence.*

Sertini in the Via de' Corsi as well as in the courtyard of the Palazzo Bartolini-Salimbeni.

Furthermore, as Vasari tells us, the facade of the Palazzo Ginori in the street of the same name was decorated by Mariano da Pescia with *Le Storie di Sansone* (The History of Samson), and Jacone painted *Le Imprese di Alessandro Magno* (The Deeds of Alexander the Great, c. 1527) on the front of the Palazzo Buondelmonti in the Piazza Santa Trinità (today completely erased). In 1553 Vasari designed a decoration with chiaroscuro figures (carried out by Cristofano Gherardi) for the facade of the Palazzo di Sforza Almeni, and in 1568 supplied a plan for ornamental graffiti for the exterior wall of the Palazzo Ramirez de Montalvo, painted in 1573 by Bernardino Poccetti and contemporary with the graffiti for the palazzo of Bianca Cappello. The figures in these decorations were the harpies, dragons, monsters, two-tailed sirens and other motifs, mainly grotesque, used by the painter from Arezzo, Alessandro Forzoni, to make more impressive the facade of the Palazzo dei Cavalieri di Santo Stefano in Pisa (1564–66). In Florence, polychrome allegories, painted in fresco in 1575, adorned the front walls of the

*Facade of the Palazzo Uguccioni, Florence.*

Palazzo Benci in the Piazza Madonna degli Aldobrandini, and of the Palazzo Mellini Fossi in the Via de' Benci. For the decoration of the latter the cartoons of Francesco de' Rossi, known as Il Salviati, were used, and it was carried out by the Dutch painter Johannes Stolf.

The fashion for facades with painted figures lasted into the 17th century. This is shown by the Palazzo dell'Antella, the front of which, overlooking the Piazza Santa Croce, was frescoed by the better painters of the time, under the direction of Giovanni da San Giovanni (1620).

Even at the time when paintings were adding color to the exteriors of Florentine palazzi, the habit of building monochrome facades of stone persisted, and at least three of them, because of their appearance and size, are unique examples, truly genuine exceptions in this urban landscape. In chronological order, the first of the three facades that are distinctly different from the usual Florentine models is that of the Palazzo Uguccioni (1550), because of the importance of the superimposition, in two orders, of pairs of twinned semi-columns, Ionic and Corinthian, that supply the vertical framework between which the background walls are framed by the window arches. Although it is true that the ashlar blocks of the first floor, with radiating stones framing the three arches, and the original continuous balcony (replaced in the 19th century by an iron balustrade) could claim some similarity with the facade of the Palazzo Pitti, nevertheless the arrangement of the two upper floors differs from that found in any other Florentine building; as a contemporary report states, the client, Giovanni Uguccioni, "had brought from Rome a design for a building that is very fine." The design, which one has to presume was similar to the facade (on two floors only above ground) of the contemporary, Roman and Raphaelesque Palazzo Vidoni Caffarelli, was translated into a wooden model by Mariotto di Zanobi Folfi, known as Ammogliato. The original roof-terrace, with a loggia standing back from the line of the facade, was an unusual solution for the Florentine region, as were the bulk and the plastic energy of the architectural members, by means of which the building, without issuing any challenge from the point of view of size, stood in counterpoint to the mass of the Palazzo Vecchio opposite, and the wide space of the adjacent Piazza della Signoria, at that time paved with brick.

On the route between the Palazzo Vecchio and the river, almost a continuation and echo of the unusual facade of the Palazzo Uguccioni, the long, solemn, and parallel facades of the Uffizi (1559–74) are atypical in form. The monumental monolithic columns and the wide pilasters of smooth stone articulate on the first floor the spans of the architraved loggia, on which is placed the crowded and overhanging modeling of the walls: the unusual "mezzanine" is pierced by open

*Painted decoration of the facade of the Palazzo Benci, Piazza Madonna degli Aldobrandini, Florence.*

Florentine attitudes: while keeping, for political purposes and to create a visible continuity of tradition, the external appearance of the palazzo, it was preferable that the expression of the ambitions and status of the owner should be confined to its interior image, kept hidden and exclusive.

When, in 1540, Cosimo I, showing great and highly visible political determination, decided to move from the Palazzo Medici in the Via Larga and chose the Palazzo Vecchio as the ducal residence, he decided also not to change the external appearance of the former seat of the priors, which was a symbol of municipal liberty, and he only made changes to the interior. Just as Cosimo the Elder had turned down the over-ambitious proposal put to him by Brunelleschi, so Cosimo I turned down the idea of a "modern palace" and, claiming that his own principate was a continuation from republican institutions, ordered that the Palazzo Vecchio should be modestly altered to fulfill its new functions, "so as not to alter the maternal foundations and walls of this place, because in its older form it had given birth to its new governor."

Giorgio Vasari, Cosimo I's trusted architect and painter, in 1555 drew up a refurbishment plan in which the second-floor quarters, to have decoration glorifying the history of the Medici, were to be used for public functions, while the third floor, ornamented with legendary themes, was to be devoted to the daily and private life of the duke's family.

For indoor public ceremonies Vasari provided the Sala Grande, then known as the Salone dei Cinquecento or Salon of the Five Hundred, and gave it a coffered ceiling, the compartments of which were decorated (1565) to an iconographical plan by Vincenzo Borghini with allegorical figures representing Tuscan cities and celebrating events in the history of Florence, crowned with an apotheosis of Cosimo I.

The walls of the Salon are painted in fresco (1567–71), showing figures related to episodes in the victorious wars against Siena and Pisa. Still on the second floor, to a commemorative program drawn up by the scholar Cosimo Bartoli, Vasari and his collaborators painted, between 1555 and 1562, the ceilings and walls of Leo X's apartment, with rooms dedicated to the famous deeds of Cosimo the Elder, Lorenzo the Magnificent, Leo X, Giovanni delle Bande Nere, Clement VII, and Cosimo I. On the third floor, in 1545, Francesco Salviati had frescoed the Audience Hall with the *Storie di Furio Camillo* (History of Furius Camillus). From 1555, under the direction of Vasari, who ordered "the brush to represent the matters of philosophical fable," the Rooms of the Elements, of Ceres, Ops, Jove, and Hercules, and the Studies of Calliope and Minerva, were decorated with allegories surrounded by grotesques, scrolls, and gargoyles. The rooms until then occupied by the gonfaloniers and the

frames that give light to the gallery and linked by extended corbels to the upper floor that is filled with windows (and balconies) separated by narrow strips of plaster. These two strong and facing curtain walls give the space between them an unusual ambiguity, making it both a street and a courtyard.

A strong "breath" of Roman influence, a rare plastic strength, expressed in the vibrant robustness of the rusticated courses that make up the superimposed semi-columns (modeled on the Porta Maggiore in Rome), the expansion and flow of the space that, originally, penetrated the second and third-floor loggias that open on to the central and lateral facades: these are the material and expressive elements of the very special characteristics of Ammannati's courtyard in the Palazzo Pitti, completed in 1577. The U-shaped plan, despite the extraordinary appearance of its vigorous facades and the views of it running down from the Boboli hill, is essentially inward-looking and to be enjoyed "in private" by the privileged few.

The exceptional characteristics of the courtyard of the Palazzo Pitti, anticipated, encouraged, and carried out by Cosimo I in order to increase the distinction of what, by 1570, was the grand ducal residence, confirm the durability of

priors were turned into the quarters of the Duchess Eleonora, and the Rooms of the Sabines, of Esther, Penelope, and Gualdrada were given frescoes representing "the deeds of famous Greek, Hebrew, Roman, and Tuscan women" (1561–62).

Much more learned, full of obscurities and complex symbols, was the iconography the fertile mind of Borghini provided for Vasari when in 1570, as an old man, he set up the *Studiolo* (Study) required by the reigning prince Francesco I that was to reflect this ruler's inward-looking habit of mind. Making use, almost as a witty play of contrast, of a small area adjacent to the enormous and public Salone dei Cinquecento (Salon of the Five Hundred), this hidden and very personal *Studiolo* was a mysterious and muffled refuge, a totally private cell, without

light from the outside, sacred to the "sweet hours" of the night and the enjoyment of "things rare and precious," both of art and nature, with which the prince liked to surround himself. To decorate this microcosm of learned marvels, to do justice to the rarities collected by the prince and carefully kept in cupboards with painted shutters, Vasari made use of a whole number of talented painters, among whom were Stradano, Poppi, Alessandro Allori, Santi di Tito, and Masso da San Friano, and well-known sculptors such as Giambologna, Ammannati, Vincenzo Danti, Stoldo Lorenzi and Vincenzo de' Rossi. The *Studiolo* of Francesco I, a precious pearl secreted in the heart of the Palazzo Vecchio, is yet another sign of the predilection of wealthy Florentines for rich and eccentric adornment of

*Painted decoration of the facade of the Palazzo Mellini-Fossi, Florence.*

*Following pages, the Salon of the Five Hundred, Palazzo Vecchio, Florence; note the great coffered wood ceiling with decorated compartments, and the frescoes on the walls by Vasari.*

41

Hercules Killing the Dragon in the Garden of the Hesperides *by Lorenzo della Sciorina, painted door pilaster of a cabinet in the Studiolo of Francesco I de'Medici, Palazzo Vecchio, Florence.*

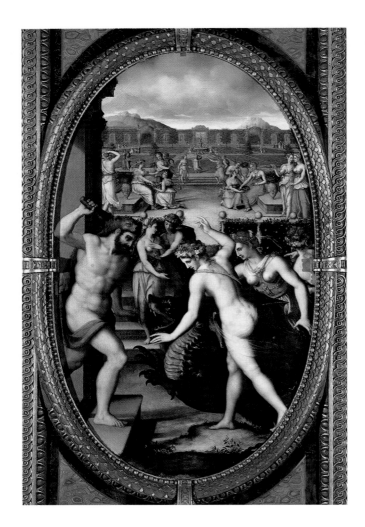

their interiors, to the prejudice of the exterior appearance of their houses.

Even when there is an outside garden reserved for the use of the privileged few, the lay-out and surrounding greenery seem to be a projection into the open air of the internal space of the palazzo, a continuation of the privacy into an imitation of nature. In fact, in Tuscany there are not many examples of private urban gardens that are worth noting for their formal qualities; among the exceptions are the small 17th-century rectangle of greenery adjacent to the Palazzo Guinigi in Florence, with its aedicule and fountain featuring giants carved out of the stone, the Garden of the Orti Oricellai (Rucellai Gardens) that is part of the Casino of Cardinal Giovanni Carlo de' Medici (later called the Palazzo Strozzi-Ridolfi) in the Via della Scala, which has a Cave of the Winds and a majestic Colossus fountain built of "brick and stucco" by the sculptor Antonio Novelli (c. 1650), and the charming small 17th-century garden, backing on to the city walls and ornamented with contemporary sculpture, that lies behind the Palazzo Moriconi (later called the Palazzo Pfanner) in Lucca.

Although the exceptional Giardino di Boboli (started in 1550) is astounding for its grandeur, geometrical flower-beds, monumental water-works, architectural features, and alley-ways of

*Detail of the vault of the Studiolo of Francesco I de'Medici, Palazzo Vecchio, Florence.*

*The Boboli Gardens, Florence: at the end of the Alley of Trees, the Isolotto pond with the Oceano fountain at its center.*

statues, it is, in fact, an extension outwards of the inside of the Palazzo Pitti that Cosimo I chose as his home and palace. On this island of domesticated nature it was decided (not without some hint of agoraphobia) to create a space even more cut off, "internal" and private, by building an alcove, or grotto, in protective rusticated stone. The *Grotticina di Madama* (1553–55) and the *Grotta Grande* (1584–87), with the fascinating ambiguity of their stalactite encrustations of calcareous and tufa stones, are excellent examples of the desire to retire into a comforting interior space.

Acceptance of the conformity of the facade on grounds of tradition, often a very real consideration, and pleasure in making a show of the finery and caprices of riches in the private confines of one's home, were the "social" considerations that in the 17th and 18th centuries still conditioned the architectural characteristics of the Tuscan palazzo, especially in Florence.

We have only to remember that, for the lateral additions to the facade of the Palazzo Pitti, both Cosimo II de' Medici in 1620, and Ferdinando II in 1631, decided, with considered

*Bottom, left, the Boboli Gardens, Florence, detail of a small fountain that is part of the elliptical Isolotto pond.*

*Bottom, right, the Boboli Gardens, Florence, the Meridiana green, with an antique statue of Marcus Aurelius (in the foreground) and an 18th-century Pegasus.*

"political" realism, to keep "the same order of architecture" as that of the original central nucleus, putting the unpretentious Giulio and Alfonso Parigi in charge of the work; but to decorate some of the rooms of the palazzo fittingly the famous Pietro da Cortona was brought from Rome in 1637. With innovative Baroque splendor he painted frescoes of the *Quattro età dell'uomo* (Four Ages of Man) in the Stanza della Stufa (Stove Room), and between 1641 and 1647 decorated the Sale dei Pianeti (Planet Rooms) with stucco work that lent some dynamic modeling to the box-like spaces of these salons. Ferdinando II, perhaps not satisfied

*Colossus Fountain by Antonio Novelli in the Orti Oricellari garden, Florence.*

with the appearance of the Medici royal palace after it had been enlarged, asked Pietro da Cortona for a plan to renew the whole facade of the Palazzo Pitti. Cortona's proposal to transfer and superimpose on the front some of the powerful compositional and formal themes of Ammannati's facade in the courtyard is in line, at least from the point of view of method, with the Florentine custom of not making a show of any excessively modern architecture on the exterior.

The Riccardi, who bought the old and prestigious Medicean residence in 1659, showed a similar conservatory caution. The new owners employed the architect Giovan Battista Foggini to extend the facade on the Via Larga by reproducing faithfully the 15th-century articulations of Michelozzo; but inside they allowed themselves the luxury and novelty of a gallery and library that were unashamedly Baroque in the abundance of their gilded stucco, also designed by Foggini, the preciosity of mirrors painted by Anton Domenico Gabbiani, and splendid ceilings decorated in fresco between 1682 and 1691 by Gabbiani, Luca Giordano, and Giuseppe and Tommaso Nasini.

On a reduced scale, the same differentiation between an insignificant exterior and a fairly ambitious interior is found in Michelangelo Buonarroti the Younger's refurbishment of the small Florentine palazzo dedicated to the memory of his uncle. In contrast to the simple facade overlooking the Via Ghibellina, the rooms of the interior were decorated with portraits of the significant personalities and events in the Buonarroti family history, the chapel and the library were embellished with pictures, and between 1615 and 1637 the walls of the gallery were hung with tapestries depicting the important events in the life of the "divine" artist, while on the ceiling were "figures… representing the power and strength of soul that, in life, made Michelangelo great and glorious: Intelligence, Talent, Study, Tolerance, Patriotism, Piety, Moderation, Honor." It is significant that in 1875, the fourth centenary of the birth of Michelangelo, the architects Corinto Corinti and Giacomo Roster, with the painters Federico Andreotti, Niccolò Barabino, Amos Cassioli, and Cosimo Conti, put forward a proposal to improve the facade of the Palazzetto Buonarroti by filling it with graffito work of symbolic figures.

Even an artist as distinguished as Giorgio Vasari acted in the same way when, having bought a house in 1541 in his native Arezzo in preparation for his marriage (which took place in 1550), he rebuilt it without giving any regard to the facade, but dedicated himself passionately, between 1542 and 1548, to the pictorial decorations of the rooms.

He frescoed the vaulted ceilings of two rooms with allegories of Reputation and the Arts, and figures of Apollo and the Muses; he painted in

*Plaster and fresco decorations by Pietro da Cortona, in the Sala di Giove of the Palazzo Pitti, Florence.*

*Study for the facade of the Palazzo Pitti, Florence, Pietro da Cortona, by Gabinetto Disegni e Stampe degli Uffizi, no. 3512 A.*

The inscription on the banner reads:

RECTORES ORBIS GENS ET PRIMORDIA RERVM
HOS FALSO FINXIT QVOS COLVIT QVE DEOS

The Creation of Man by *Luca Giordano, detail of the frescoed ceiling in the Gallery of the Palazzo Medici-Riccardi, Florence.*

tempera the coffered ceiling of the wedding chamber, the so-called Abraham room, and in the large living room, which had a monumental stone fireplace, he represented on the walls and wood ceiling the *Trionfo della Virtù* (Triumph of Virtue) and the *Primato dell'Arte* (Supremacy of Art), framing the allegorical images with simulated caryatids, grotesque gargoyles, and painted curtains and festoons.

Returning to Florence and the fact already established, by reference to the Palazzi Pitti and Medici-Riccardi, that the external value of the houses of notable citizens lay primarily in the long rows of windows that indicated the wealth of their owners, we find clear confirmation of this "indicator" in the facades of other large residential buildings such as the Palazzi Pucci in the street of the same name, Roffia in the Borgo Pinti, Panciatichi in the Via Larga, Marucelli in

the Via San Gallo, Guadagni in the Piazza del Duomo, Incontri in the Via de' Servi, and Orlandini in the Via de' Pecori. The great number of windows in each of these buildings was the result of an easily achieved surface rehabilitation, which joined together in a single facade the fronts of the adjacent buildings that families, rising in social rank, bought in order to enlarge original homes that were no longer appropriate for their new situation.

The common practice, arising from restraint and thrift, was to join up and reorganize the different facades as simply as possible by realigning the openings on the various floors. In other words, the facade retained the appearance of a more or less continuous wall, a more or less solid barrier protecting the interior. The only architectural element added to these 17th and 18th-century palazzi in an attempt to try and

with views that widen out towards the river. The 18th-century Palazzo Capponi, in addition to the theatrical main staircase decorated with "antique and modern statues," a fountain, and ceiling frescoes by Marco Bonechi, has an Italian garden leading to a charming orangery, the facade of which is encrusted with colored *rocailles*.

Similar in some respects to the Palazzo Corsini is the Palazzo Cybo Malaspina in Massa. This building, which became a ducal residence in 1664, and has a theater, a library, a chapel, a garden, and a grotto with three naves, faces towards the main piazza of the town for the full length of its facade, which, rebuilt at the beginning of the 18th century to a plan by Alessandro Bergamini, has exuberant decoration around the windows and is colored red. The most spectacular architectural effects, however, are the airy staircase in front of it, the three sides of the loggia with a double order of columns and terraces edged with balustrades, and, especially, the cross-section of the belvedere loggia, doubled and "transparent," from which there is a magnificent

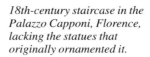

*18th-century staircase in the Palazzo Capponi, Florence, lacking the statues that originally ornamented it.*

*Example of the small parapets on the facade of the Palazzo Corsini in Castello.*

break up the wearisome uniformity of facade, and which accentuated the importance of its central axis, was the "poggioletto," or small balcony, a secular arch over the main entrance consisting of a vertical sequence of a projecting portico, surmounted by a small balcony, linked to a French window that was in turn surmounted by the family coat of arms; a sequence that was to become a decorative cliché and a sure sign of a lack of creative ideas.

Inside the palazzi, however, in further proof of the adoption of the double standard in the language of form that provided for simple solutions for the composition of facades and more elaborate and up-to-date solutions for internal furbishment, there were majestic staircases ornamented with statues, rows of galleries on the *piano nobile*, entertainment rooms with continuous balconies running round them, picture galleries, alcoves and chapels heavy with stucco and gilding, frescoed walls and ceilings that were virtually made larger by the perspective effects of the painting, grottoes populated with legendary figures, all indicating the desire to be different and make a show, and the adjustment of the Florentine aristocracy (not such by "birth and the sword," but by trade) to the flattering dictates of first Spanish, and then French fashion.

Two attractive summaries of these internal attributes can be seen in the Palazzo Capponi, in the then Via San Sebastiano behind the church of SS. Annunziata, and in the Palazzo Corsini, in the street of the same name that runs parallel with the Arno. The Palazzo Corsini, built between 1656 and 1737, because of its U-shaped plan and the loggias and terraces of various sizes that open on its facades, can boast of an exceptional outlook,

*Detail of the facade of the Palazzo Ducale, Massa.*

view of the horizon with the sea in the distance. It is not surprising that the court poet Nicolò Margaritoni should describe so enthusiastically the spaces and marbles "that form a charming labyrinth of columns and are the greatest pleasure to be found in the royal palace of the Cybi."

In the 17th century the many and detailed descriptions and illustrations of the history and art of the larger Tuscan cities (the precursors of today's "guides") already tended to put a high value on the contemporary and better architectural achievements, giving particular attention to the palazzi built by important local families. Although in the 18th century there was a veritable publicity campaign for the beauty of the cities, waged by means of prints (such as those designed for Florence by Giuseppe Zocchi in 1744), which intentionally exaggerated the size of the streets and piazze and glorified the magnificence of the usual "fetish" monuments, nevertheless the

*Palazzo Ducale, Massa: one of the twin staircase ramps leading from the courtyard to the loggia/belvedere level.*

opinions of foreign travelers about the architecture of the Tuscan and Florentine palazzi were not all indulgent. The simplicity of the forms was appreciated as a positive quality, as the Englishman, Pierre Jean Grosley, noted during his visit to Italy in 1764: "Among private Florentine buildings the palazzo built by the first Medici has pride of place; not for the size of the space it occupies… but for its elegant simplicity." Rather similarly Jacob Burckhardt wrote in 1878 that the Florentine palazzo is "an impressive palace in stone, the appearance of which is based on the narrow range and strength of its individual elements." Thirty years later, in 1907, Charles Edouard Jeanneret (the future Le Corbusier) described the 13th-century Bargello as "one of the ancient severe palaces of the XVth century [sic!], architecturally both powerful and simple."

After the simplicity, it was the rusticated stone, or the embattled appearance of many palazzi, that caught the attention of many travelers. Referring to the Palazzo Medici, the Englishman Edward Gibbon wrote in 1764: "This house is of the rusticated architecture so common in Florence and which gives the palaces the appearance of fortresses. At one time it was necessary that it should be such."

In 1817 Stendhal said: "It is clear from the solidity of these palaces built with enormous stone blocks that are rough on the side that faces the street, that danger has often passed this way." In 1837 the American James Fenimore Cooper expressed the opinion that "the feuds between

*Orangery in the garden of the Palazzo Capponi, Florence.*

*Palazzo Corsini, Florence: room on the first floor with "grotto" designed by Carlo Marcellini.*

51

*Palazzo Pitti, Florence: salon on the first floor with wall decorations by Michelangelo Colonna and Agostino Mitelli showing* trompe-l'œil *architectural perspectives ("paneling").*

the factions gave rise to a kind of architecture that is almost exclusively Florentine, every palace is in fact a fortress."

John Ruskin, a fanatical admirer of Gothic refinement, said in 1840 that he hated "the palaces that look like prisons," and the Frenchman Hippolyte Taine wrote in 1864: "the old palaces built of enormous stones, with their rough rusticated ashlar, their windows bristling with ironwork, their angles grim and blackened, tell of the dangers of medieval life and the attacks made upon them."

Simplicity combined with rusticated stone blocks gave a feeling of uniformity to the facades of the palazzi. This was the impression of the Burgundian Charles de Brosses, who stated in 1739: "The palaces of Florence are many and famous. However, they do not convince me fully. The architecture of almost all of them is rusticated, flat and uniform."

Even more severe was Théophile Gautier's comment on Florence: "This city… is boring and gloomy in appearance, and its palaces look like prisons." Something similar was said by the Bohemian Rainer Maria Rilke in his *Florentine Diary* (1898): "the palaces lift their mute facades against the foreigner in hostility," facades characterized by "militaristic and suspicious faces"; "the windows that break this heavy silence are few and mean, fearful of letting slip something of the feeling that animates these walls." It is worth noting that de Brosses spoke about the Palazzo Vecchio in these words: "it is nothing but an old Bastille, surmounted by a large and ugly tower. It is as dark and gloomy on the inside as it is on the outside." Returning from Siena, the young Le Corbusier found the Palazzo Vecchio "heavy and coarse," "old and gloomy"; although he later admits: "one does not know how to get at its mystery. It is disturbing, there are quite refined touches on its ugly facade, some strength in its tower" and, "It is a great marvel, but it is difficult to study it, it is an abstract power."

A more conciliatory judgment was expressed by the Marquis de Sade, who, passing through Florence in 1775, had this to say of the city: "It is full of grand buildings, but in the Gothic style and little pleasing to the eye, since the finest palaces are rusticated and built of a brown stone that gives them a sullen appearance. The ancient windows and the prodigious height are both elements that do not contribute to a pleasing effect; but they are nevertheless very noble and magnificent."

A short but exact comment was made by the English priest Alban Butler in 1746: "The palaces of Florence are majestic, but more so on the inside than the outside." A realistic analysis, showing some enthusiasm, was made by the American writer Henry James in his *Italian Hours* of 1909, and later in *Florence Revisited*:

*The more I look at the old Florentine domestic architecture the more I like it… if I ever am able to build myself a lordly pleasure-house I don't see how in conscience I can build it differently from these. They are somber and frowning, and look a trifle more as if they were meant to keep people out than to let them in; but what equally 'important' type – if there be an equally important – is more expressive of the domiciliary dignity and security and yet attests them with a finer aesthetic economy? They are impressively 'handsome', and yet contrive to be so by the simplest means… I am afraid that behind these so gravely harmonious fronts there is a good deal of dusky discomfort, and I speak now of the large serious faces themselves as you can see them from the street; see them ranged cheek by cheek in the gray historic light of Via dei Bardi, Via Maggio, Via degli Albizzi. The force of character, the familiar severity and majesty, depend on a few simple features: on the great iron-caged windows of the rough-hewn basement; on the noble stretch of space between the summit of one high, round-topped window and the bottom of that above; on the high-hung shield at the angle of the house; on the flat far-projecting roof; and, finally, on the magnificent tallness of the whole building, which dwarfs so our modern attempts at size.*

In *Florence Revisited* James draws another portrait of the charm of Florence, which, according to him, comes *from the generous aspect of those high-based Tuscan palaces which a renewal of acquaintance with them has again commended to me as the most dignified dwellings in the world. Nothing can be finer than that look of giving up the whole ground-floor to simple purposes of vestibule and staircase, of court and high-arched entrance; as if this were all but a massive pedestal for the real habitation, and people were not properly housed unless, to begin with, they should be lifted fifty feet above the pavement. The grand blocks of the basement; the great intervals, horizontally and vertically, from window to window (telling of the height and the breadth of the rooms within); the armorial shield hung forward at one of the angles; the wide-brimmed roof, overshadowing the narrow street; the rich old browns and yellows of the walls – these definite elements are put together with admirable art.*

With regard to individual buildings, it is to the point to quote what de Sade writes: "the most magnificent is the Palazzo Pitti… this rusticated architecture has something of nobility… The Palazzi Gerini, Capponi, Strozzi, and Corsini seemed to me the finest in the city. But one house, despite its simplicity, well worth visiting is that of Michelangelo… The Buonarroti, descendants of this famous artist, consider it a pleasure to show you round. The gallery is adorned with paintings by great masters showing scenes from Michelangelo's life." The adventurous marquis, while admitting that the Palazzo Riccardi "is a fine building, and speaks greatness," does not,

however, fail to comment on the meanness of the Florentine aristocracy "who are not particularly rich, or perhaps are just thrifty, live a very retired life, and never offer you a glass of water, however good your letters of recommendation."

Ruskin also noted that he had visited "with pleasure" the Buonarroti house, which "is looked after with great care," whereas Gibbon preferred to linger over the Palazzo Corsini, which "is beautiful… but has that usual and modern beauty that lacks any grandeur… The facade facing the river is very fine; there are two large and separate buildings that are unified by a terrace, but on the other hand you have to seek in a dark and narrow street [the Via del Parione] a facade that says nothing, and offers no invitation to a fine stair-case that is hidden."

Although de Brosses describes the Palazzo Medici-Riccardi as "built entirely in rusticated stone by Michelozzo… the courtyard has columns… and the walls are scattered with well-organized antique inscriptions, and the apartments are boring because they are so large… the gallery was painted by Luca Giordano; it is the main room of the Palazzo because of a number of cupboards full of bronzes… and a wonderful number of fine cameos and antique engraved stones," Herman Melville, in 1857, merely calls the same palazzo "an enormous pile, rich in arches, in poor condition, with a massive over-hanging cornice."

There are not many references to the palazzi of other Tuscan cities in the literature of the Grand Tour, but it is worth noting that the waspish de Brosses says of the Palazzo Pubblico of Siena: "It is an old building, but there is nothing notable or in the least interesting about it, except some paintings that are older and even uglier than the building itself."

Ruskin spoke better of Sienese architecture: "This city is worth fifty Florences; the buildings are generally large and solid, and have a large number of trefoil windows in the Venetian style." Of Siena the young Le Corbusier wrote to his parents: "Between the Piazza della Signoria [sic. Piazza della Signoria is in Florence, Piazza del Campo is in Siena], where the Palazzo Comunale with the famous tower stands, and the Piazza del Duomo, are almost all the best medieval palaces, epic and solemn, and nonetheless aristocratic and delicate."

Ruskin, staying in Lucca in 1845, admired the Palazzo Guinigi, which he described as an example of the noble "simplicity and strength" of domestic Italian Gothic, and the tower that he judged to be "a true and proper fortress… covered with vegetation"; he also noticed "along the street opposite… the iron rings to which horses were tethered, and the hooks from which silk flags were hung on feast days."

In *Excursions in Italy* Cooper said of the Palazzo Ducale of Lucca – "a long building,

*Opposite, the Chapel, or "Room of the Angels," in the Casa Buonarroti, Florence: ceiling and wall decoration by Jacopo Vignali and Michelangiolo Cinganelli.*

*Detail of plaster decoration in a 19th-century salon of the Palazzo Borghese, Florence.*

*19th-century bedroom alcove in the Palazzo Pannocchieschi d'Elci, Siena.*

55

without decoration, right in the center of the city" – which was then lived in by Elisa Baciocchi, Napoleon's sister, and had been rebuilt internally by the architect Lorenzo Nottolini: "I believe the palace reflects the taste and wealth of the imperial princess. The style and manner in which it is arranged we consider Parisian."

The echoes of Parisian elegance, or would-be imitation of it, were also to be found in the sumptuous furbishment with shining marbles, gilded stucco, mirrors and lamp stands, of the neo-classical Palazzi Bianchi Bandinelli in Siena and Borghese in Florence.

Giulio Bianchi Bandinelli, governor of the city and state of Siena, completed the decoration of his residence on the Via Roma in 1804, by giving it a chapel and a theater, and by having Luigi Ademollo fresco the ceilings of some of the rooms. The Napoleonic prince, Don Camillo Borghese, the separated husband of Pauline Bonaparte, sister of Napoleon built his opulent Florentine house in the Via Ghibellina to a plan by the architect Gaetano Baccani: a long facade with the usual rusticated basement, and on the *piano nobile* a loggia with Ionic columns, surmounted by a pediment with the family arms flanked by allegorical figures of the Arno and the Tiber.

In connection with the building of municipal palazzi we have only to note the inauguration in September 1922 of the massive and eclectically neo-16th-century Palazzo Comunale of Montecatini Terme, planned by Raffaello Brizzi and Luigi Arrighetti, and decorated internally with murals by Galileo Chini.

The Palazzo Borghese marked the end of the period of building large and sumptuous private dwellings in Tuscany, because, from the middle of the 19th century, the old aristocratic families and those that had recently attained to riches thought it better to place their capital in commercial and financial undertakings in the city, or, even better, in building and urban development, where profits were mainly to be made. The exploitation on capitalist principles of urban potential (speculation in factory sites, the expansion of the building market), with the movement to new and expanding residential areas both inside and outside the "historic center" (one thinks of the extensions for Florence when it became the capital of Italy and the subsequent "clearance" of the Mercato Vecchio, or Old Market, and the Ghetto), was also the signal in other Tuscan cities of the end of the monumental building belonging to a single family. No longer, then, are there grand palazzi, but prosaic apartment buildings for letting, or tiny houses and villas – products of lesser ambition – located in the inner suburbs.

The individual seigniorial palace of the past has been overtaken by the commonplace "condominium," a one-floor micro-palazzo to satisfy the modest aspirations of so many micro-owners.

*The neo-classical "Statues Gallery" in the Palazzo Ducale, Lucca.*

CLAUDIO RENDINA

# THE PALAZZI OF FLORENCE AND TUSCANY

# PALAZZO PUBBLICO, SIENA

*View of the Palazzo Pubblico, Siena, overlooking the historic Piazza del Campo, with the Torre del Mangia and, on the left, the Cappella di Piazza.*

The back-drop to this palazzo, the Campo, is its own *raison d'être*; the magnificent Siena piazza, designed as an amphitheater for festivals, tournaments and entertainments, of which the Palio (the famous horse-race) is the most notable, reflects the public life of the city in its strategic positioning and in the brick paving that make it an urban center *par excellence*. It is a stage on which for centuries the Sienese have met for civil and religious celebrations, but where governments have also demonstrated their power to settle in the light of day disputes of a public nature; in the spring of 1315, for example, when faced with bloody strife between the Salimbeni and Tolomei families, the Nine, representatives of the Guelph governor of the day, "placed a candle outside the Palazzo Pubblico, declaring that if the two families did not make peace by the time the candle burned out, their persons and goods would all be seized."

The Campo, finished on 11 March 1169 and sited on an area of land bought by the notables of the Municipality, provided an incentive for them to build a Palazzo for the commune. A decision to build was taken in 1288, when the magistrates, tired of meeting in churches, houses, and towers, issued a decree that provided for the preparation of a plan. At first work began on rebuilding the Customs House, already located on the piazza and housing the *podestà*, or chief magistrate, and the *consiglia della campana*, or Tower Council; then a change was made. In 1293 some houses surrounding the Customs House were bought to make expansion possible, and in 1297 a committee of twelve citizens was appointed to decide upon a plan and the building procedure. Between 1298 and 1310 the central part of the palazzo was built: the first floor, in stone, was measured out in ten Sienese arches; the second, in brick, was articulated with triple-mullioned windows; the tower had triple-mullioned windows on the third floor and twin-mullioned windows on the fourth, and it was surmounted by an arched campanile.

The Nine, wishing to win enduring fame for their political program, decided to paint in fresco the still unfinished rooms, and entrusted the work to

*On the following pages, a panoramic view of Siena showing, in the foreground, the Campo, the square that symbolizes the city and around which a number of noble buildings rise; the most magnificent of these being the Palazzo Pubblico.*

*Opposite, the Courtyard of the Podestà, which is entirely in brick, surrounded by a portico surmounted by large triple-mullioned windows with pointed arches.*

*Detail of the facade of the palazzo, showing the arches of the first floor and the triple-mullioned windows of the two upper floors; right, detail of the interior of the portico in the courtyard.*

Sienese masters; thus the masterpieces that were to constitute the Civic Museum were created.

The central part of the palazzo was hardly completed before a historic event took place there on 10 May 1321. Messer Biagio de' Montanigio gave a lecture on the legal aspects of the civic value of art and culture. Present at this were a number of professors and students from Bologna who, no longer able to tolerate the oppressive interference of politicians, had left their university and fled to Siena, seeking a kind of political asylum and membership of the Sienese Athenaeum.

Work continued, and in 1325 the residence of the *podestà* was extended; behind this addition, between 1327 and 1330, the prison was built, which until then had been located in the cellars of the Palazzo Pannocchieschi d'Elci, then owned by the Cerretani. On the floor above the prison came the Chamber of the Gran Consiglio della Repubblica (Great Council of the Republic); the first meeting was held in 1343.

The development of the palazzo on its right side had made it asymmetrical, but this was put right by

the building of the Tower, which rose to a height of 102 meters from 1325 on under the direction of Minuccio and Francesco di Rinaldo, two master builders from Perugia. There are 332 steps to the belfry, from where the master bell, known as the "sunta" because it is dedicated to Maria Assunta, has sounded out the hours of Siena's history up to the present day. This is the Torre del Mangia, called after the first bell-ringer, Bartolomeo Ducci, nicknamed "Mangiaguadagni" (eats-what-he-earns), who, when he died, was replaced by a mechanical wooden figure that inherited the small stature of the ringer, then by a brass one, and, in 1759, by one in travertine. This worked until 1780, when it was removed to the cellars of the palazzo and subsequently disappeared. The archaeologist Ranuccio Bianchi Bandinelli discovered it in 1924 in a family villa in Pagliaia, then owned by the Liccioli, who agreed to his returning it to the Municipality, which placed it in the courtyard of the *podestà*.

The Cappella della Piazza, dedicated to the Virgin, was built at the foot of the Torre; it was the fruit of a vow made during the terrible plague of 1348, but work only began in 1352, paid for by the Opera del Duomo and private donations. The Municipality presented it with four candlesticks. It appears that the architectural design, attributed to Domenico d'Agostino, did not please the Sienese, so it became a work of many hands; in a series of revisions and reversals over a long period, it was carried out by two different builders, its columns with statues of the saints being by three sculptors working between 1375 and 1427. The ceiling with

*Above, detail of the*
Virgin in Majesty
*by Simone Martini
in the Map Room,
painted in 1315 and
probably the richest
evidence we have of
Sienese Gothic art.*

*Right, detail of the
fresco of 1338 showing*
The Effects of Good
Government, *the work
of Ambrogio Lorenzetti
in the Room of Peace,
also known as the
Room of the
Crossbows.*

*Opposite, a corner of
the Room of the
Aldermen, with
frescoes showing*
Scenes from the Life of
Pope Alexander III, *the
Sienese Rolando
Bandinelli Paparoni,
painted by Spinello
Aretino (about 1408).*

SANCTA CATHARINA SENENSIS

HIPPV

*Opposite, the walls of the former Cancelle della Biccherna (the seat of financial administration in Siena), with a fresco dating from about 1445 showing the* The Coronation of the Virgin *by Sano di Pietro and Domenico di Bartolo, and, left, detail of an angel.*

*Below, a wall in the Stanza della Biccherna, with a fresco, attributed to Antonio Gregori, above the door showing* The Departure of Maria de' Medici as the Betrothed of Henry IV of France, *dated about 1601.*

*Above, the large fresco by Simone Martini in the Sala del Mappamondo, showing* Giudoriccio da Fogliano, *the Sienese general at the siege of Montemassi.*

*Right, this fresco, by a Sienese artist of the first half of the 14th century, perhaps Duccio di Buoninsegna, is in the Sala del Mappamondo, immediately under the fresco of* Giudoriccio da Fogliano, *and shows* The Peaceful Surrender to Siena of a Fortified Town, *a work datable to c. 1314.*

*Far right,* Peace and War, *detail of* The Effects of Good Government, *a fresco of the years 1337–40 by Ambrogio Lorenzetti in the Sala della Pace.*

*Opposite, one of the two 14th-century wolves, worn away by time; gargoyle spouts attributed to Giovanni Pisano, now brought inside and preserved in the central area at Campo level.*

its frieze is from 1468, and the marble statues, two of which were remade in 1846, were taken from the ancient font of the cathedral. The fresco, now in poor condition, was painted by Sodoma in 1538.

By then a number of alterations had been made to the facade, culminating in the great copper disk of a radiant sun with the monogram of Christ, IHS, invented by St. Bernardino of Siena: a tribute to the saintly exorcist and the help he and his twelve volunteers had given the population during the latest of numerous epidemics of 1423. The work,

Sala del Consiglio: it became a theater in 1561, and was linked with the activities of the Accademia degli Intronati, a literary academy founded in the 16th century. It was to be destroyed twice by fire, but rebuilt in 1753 by Antonio Bibbiena, to become the Teatro Comunale dei Rinnovati, and restored again in 1951. But it was the 17th century that saw the main alterations to the palazzo: a third floor was placed on the side wings, similar to the second, and a vestibule and staircase were built. Additions were made to the interior in the 19th century that,

*Above, a portal in the Sala del Cantino (formerly the Room of the Consistory) by Bernardo Rossellino. On the right, the* Acca Larentia, *from the* Fount of Joy *by Jacopo della Quercia, removed from the Campo in the 19th century.*

embossed by the Paduan Battista di Niccolò, its rays made by Turino di Sano and his son Giovanni, was installed in 1425. Turino also made the gilded bronze she-wolf, the city's emblem, that was once at the entrance to the rooms of the Signoria, where there is now a copy, the original being inside.

After the fall of the Republic, the palazzo underwent a number of changes, starting with the

to mirror a Siena that was now part of a unified Italy, tried to link the emblem of the "good governor" of the Republic with that of the Savoyard king in the Sala del Risorgimento; it is a work that is totally out of keeping in the context of a palazzo celebrated as an image of Siena from the 13th to the 17th centuries. The masterpieces in the Civic Museum are largely a testimony to the

PATRIE AMOR

CARYNDAS
TIRORVM
PRINCEPS

CELIVS
PRAETOR

CODRVS
REX
ATHENIEN
SIVM

GENVTIVS·
CIPPVS·
PRÆTOR·

The ceiling of the Vaulted
Room, with fresco allegories by
Domenico Beccafumi. In
particular, in the center of the
ceiling, the Allegory of
Patriotism of 1529.

75

*Opposite, the Sala del Risorgimento, the last large painting project carried out in the Palazzo Pubblico, by Sienese artists such as Cesare Maccari and Pietro Aldi, with statues and marble busts by Emilio Gallori and Tito Sarrocci.*

wisdom and good taste of the ruling classes of those centuries.

To start with, there was, in the Sala del Mappamondo, the *Maestà* of Simone Martini, painted in 1315, a "portrait of Our Lady" intended to advise the citizens gathered in the room beneath it to govern justly, directing them:

Again, in the fresco cycle *Buono e cattivo governo* (Good and Bad Government) painted by

of power. The message of the Palazzo Pubblico speaks down the centuries at the dawn of the third millennium through the architecture and the works of art it contains, and is summed up in the verses of the epigraph of the *Effetti del buon governo* (The Effects of Good Government):

"My dears, remember / during your humble and honest prayers, / if you want me to speak for you / that, if the powerful injure the weak / causing them

*Above, detail of a fresco in the Sala del Risorgimento by Cesare Maccari showing* The Presentation to Vittorio Emanuele of the Roman Plebiscite *(1886).*

Ambrogio Lorenzetti between 1337 and 1339 in the old Sala dei Signori, there is a strong peace message, given through a series of extraordinary historic significance: in the clashes between the figures of rebellion, vanity, discord, avarice, pride, and vainglory, images of unusual historical weight are given that even today evoke violence and abuse

pain and suffering / your prayers will not help these evil doers / and not those who, on my and, trick and deceive".

NON LA DESTATE

# PALAZZO NUOVO DEL PODESTÀ DEL COMUNE, SAN GIMIGNANO

*Opposite, the Cathedral and the Palazzo del Comune or Palazzo Nuovo del Podestà.*

"You feel more as if you are in a courtyard than in a street. Even the squares are courtyards, and in all of them, you feel sheltered." Thus wrote Walter Benjamin as he traveled through San Gimignano, a medieval island set well away from hectic modern life and where one instinctively feels taken back in time. The magic is created by the visual impact of the towers which, in the 14th century, numbered as many as 72, a veritable forest, and of which now only 15 remain, but still offer a superb panorama from the 54 meters high Torre Grossa which rises above the Palazzo del Comune (City Hall).

Since 1288, when it rose as the Palazzo Nuovo (new palazzo) of the *podestà*, the tower has dominated the south side of the cathedral square. Previously, from 1239 on, he had used offices on the opposite side of the square, from which rises yet another, slightly shorter tower, the Rognosa. This, however, was abandoned after 1358 when it was designated for use by ambassadors to the Commune. The Palazzo Nuovo meanwhile would be witness to

*General view of the north side of the Piazza del Duomo, San Gimignano, with, on the left, the twin towers of the Palazzo dei Salvucci, formerly Patroni, which give the square a great deal of its character.*

78

Opposite bottom, view of the Sala del Consiglio, known as the Dante Room, because this was where the great poet was welcomed, showing a coffered ceiling and, on the walls at the back, the fresco Virgin in Majesty by Lippo Memmi of 1317, representing the Madonna and Child with angels and saints and the Podestà Nello di Mino de' Tolomei.

The courtyard of the palazzo with its bare medieval porticoes.

*Two crucifixes on the sides of the entrance to the salon of the Pinacoteca: right, the* Crucifix with the Mourning Prophets Isaiah and Jeremiah and the Redeemer Giving His Blessing *(c. 1280–85), attributed to the Master of the Poor Clares, and, left, the* Crucifix with Scenes of the Passion *by Coppo di Marcovaldo (c. 1255–60), a 13th-century masterpiece.*

the history of the city, from the adventures of the Guelphs and the Ghibellines to its involvement in medieval Tuscany, the Lorraine, and eventually Italy.

The palazzo is symbolized by the Torre Grossa itself where the *podestà* lived, successively governing the city and adding their coats of arms as the tower grew higher and higher. The most notable historical event to take place during its early phase was the ambassadorship of Dante Alighieri, who was invited by the Florentines to San Gimignano to plead for a sorely needed Tuscan–Guelph league. On 8 May 1300 Dante's voice rang through the halls of the palazzo as he tried in vain to persuade the *podestà* and the General Council to send citizens to the Taglia Guelfa Commune parliament to elect a captain. This hall is called the Sala di Dante and now forms part of the Civic Museum. Founded in 1852, it houses the Filippo Menni *Maestà* of 1317, with its Madonna and Child among Angels and Saints and showing the *podestà* of the time, Nello di Mino de' Tolomei.

The palazzo was extended to the back in 1323, with a courtyard, and a twin-ramp external staircase giving on to the public square were added. The tower received the addition of a small bell-tower with three bells which were used to call the people at harvest time. It was within these walls that the echoes of civil strife, such as that between the Ardinghelli Guelphs and the Salvucci Ghibellines, resounded; it was here, in 1325, that the decision was taken to join the Guelph league against the warlord Castruccio Castracani; here where the order was given to confiscate the Ardinghelli houses so the loggia could be built in 1338; and finally, it was here in 1348 that the problems of plague and famine had to be faced which would mark the decline of the Commune. Eventually, in 1351, San Gimignano gave up the independent part it had played in Tuscan politics and resigned itself to serving Florence.

Since that time, the halls of the palazzo have not witnessed any historically important events,

*Large altarpiece showing* The Ascended Madonna with the Saints Pope Gregory the Great and Benedict *by Bernardino di Betto, known as Pinturicchio; documents date it to 1551.*

Madonna and Child, with Two Angels and the Saints John the Baptist, Mary Magdalene, Augustine and Martha, *tempera on wood by Benozzo Gozzoli, signed and dated 1466.*

*Detail of* A Young Man's Initiation in Love *in the Camera del Podestà, an early 14th-century fresco by Memmo di Filippuccio on two walls, showing the love life of two young people, from courtship to marriage.*

84

*The window-side wall of the Camera del Podestà, with further wedding scenes by Memmo di Filippuccio.*

nor have they changed particularly, except in 1475 when the Sala delle Adunanze was embellished with carved, inlaid chairs. Gradually, through lack of upkeep, the building fell into decline until 1882, when restoration work under the architect Giuseppe Partini led to the crowning of the complex with some Guelph-style crenellations which altered the original appearance of the building somewhat artificially.

What makes the interior of the building very special are the 13th-century decorative paintings of hunting and jousting scenes and castles. These ensure that the original medieval atmosphere of the palazzo is kept alive. There is also the exceedingly fine art gallery, the Pinacoteca, with its outstanding collection of 15th-century Sienese and Florentine paintings.

# PALAZZO VECCHIO, FLORENCE

*Opposite, view of the Palazzo Vecchio on the Piazza della Signoria, the facade, entirely of rusticated stone, surmounted by a galleried walkway. At the sides of the entrance, a copy of Michelangelo's* David *and, on the right,* Hercules and Cacus *by Baccio Bandinelli. On the left of the palazzo,* The Fountain of Neptune *known as the Biancone.*

Originally, the palazzo was not called Vecchio, meaning old, but Pubblico, having come into being to house the gonfaloniers and priors, the lawmakers of the city and the council of the republic. Later, during oligarchic times, it was used by the lords of the city, becoming the ducal palace, called Palazzo della Signoria, after 1540 when the Medici moved there. They used it as their seat of government until 1567 when they moved to the Palazzo Pitti. It was then referred to as the Palazzo Vecchio and became a symbol of past times, of republican freedom and also of absolute rule.

The palazzo was built by Arnolfo di Cambio and called the Palagio del Popolo, or the palace of the people, and rose somewhat proud and forbidding on the town square which had been cleared of houses and Ghibelline towers. The strong stone facade had twin-light mullioned windows and was crowned by a gallery that jutted out with Guelph-style corbels and crenellations, topped by a superb tower. The priors and gonfaloniers entered its doors for the first time in 1299, even before the building was finished. Work carried on uninterrupted during the lively battles between the White and the Black Guelphs. As magistrates, the priors were obliged to live in the building, so they found themselves unarmed, right in the middle of the mêlée, as they represented the various parties among the city's tradesmen and artisans. The Blacks of Corso Donati continually assailed the palace, attempting to take it, while the Whites of Vieri dei Cerchi defended the freedom of the city.

*The Palazzo Vecchio seen from the Piazzale degli Uffizi, and, right, a detail of two marble sea-horses that make up the team represented on the Biancone.*

The delightful Putto with
Dolphin, a copy of a bronze
by Andrea del Verrocchio
(c. 1470), on the fountain in the
courtyard of the Palazzo
Vecchio.

In the meantime, the building was completed
and topped with Ghibelline crenellations, a white
lily (the emblem of the city), and two bells. Every
now and then, the great walls had to be repaired as
they were damaged by the battling citizens.

Taking advantage of the divided city, Walter of
Brienne, duke of Athens and count of Lecce, and
his armed men took the Palagio on 8 September
1342. They beat down the doors with axes and
chased away the priors. The duke set himself up as
the lord of the palace, which he turned into a veritable fortress, adding vestibules and a keep and
covering the ground-floor windows with iron
grilles. It was all to no avail. On 26 July 1343,
under assault from all sides, he was forced out of
the palace as the city's people came together to
fight against his tyranny, which they quickly
brought to an end, bringing back the priors and the
gonfaloniers.

The walls were repaired yet again and a clock
was installed on the tower. Made by Nicolao da
San Frediano from Asti, it began to ring the hours
on 25 March 1353. Twenty years later, the bell was
replaced by a much bigger one that could be heard
13 miles away. A group of bell-ringers was taken
on permanently and paid. One of these was the poet
Antonio Pucci (1310–88) who set Giovanni Villani's
*Cronica* to verse and gave it the new title of

Detail of the courtyard of the
palazzo, started by Michelozzo
in the 15th century and later
added to by Vasari: the
columns were covered with
sumptuous gilt stucco, the
vaults were frescoed with
grotesques, and the walls were
decorated with views of the
most important cities of the
Austrian Empire. In the center,
Andrea del Verrocchio's
fountain.

*Decorative details in the
Salone dei Cinquecento; top,
some of the 14th-century
ceiling coffers, and, bottom, a
detail of the wall fresco* The
Emperor Maximilian Raising
the Siege of Leghorn, *painted
by Vasari between 1563 and
1565. The cycle of frescoes by
Giorgio Vasari in this salon has
as its theme the glorification of
the deeds of the Medici.*

The Spirit of Victory *in the Salone dei Cinquecento, a marble statue by Michelangelo Buonarroti from the second or third decade of the 16th century.*

*Opposite, the Studiolo di Francesco I, built under the direction of Vasari between 1570 and 1573, with a decorative scheme by Borghini. This small, dark space with a barrel vault was designed as a study for Francesco I and a place for the display of his collection of rare minerals and natural curiosities. In the background, in the lunette the* Portrait of Eleonora of Toledo *by Bronzino.*

*Centiloquio.* He was also a sort of town crier, announcing what the priors were doing in government as he went through the streets.

In 1376, construction began on a loggia in front of the Palagio. Although the building looks like an extension, it is actually free-standing. Vasari has it that Andrea di Cione Orcagna was behind the design and indeed, despite the architect's already being dead in 1368, the building carried his name for a considerable while. It would also be called the Loggia de Lanzi because a company of German mercenaries (Landsknechts) stood guard there during the time of Cosimo I. Whatever the case may be, construction finished in 1382 and the names of the elected priors and gonfaloniers who would govern the city were proclaimed to the people from here. Now it is an open-air museum for works of sculpture, including Benvenuto Cellini's famous *Perseus*.

Meanwhile, the square in front of the palace was also taking shape. The initial paving consisted of herringbone tiles and would set the stage for endless fights, most of which were in some way connected with the palace. The first of these, on 22 July 1378, involved the Ciompi, or the wool workers, led by Michele di Lando, a wool carder. The chronicles of the time record that he entered the palace shoeless and wearing little other than a gonfalonier banner, demanding along with his companions that the city be governed his way. The plan backfired though and only ended up strengthening the authority of the commune. Ironically, Michele would himself be among those to put down the revolt one month later.

If the end of the 14th century heard the squares of Florence resounding to the various factions fighting each other for power, so would the first years of the 15th. Bankers and merchants with an eye to their own interests tried more or less openly to place themselves, or their representatives, in positions of power. It was on 7 September 1433, during one of these fights for supremacy, that Cosimo de' Medici the Elder found himself imprisoned in the Alberghettino, a cell in the tower. He was accused of attempting to set up a government controlled by a few selected magistrates. As Macchiavelli wrote in his *Istorie Fiorentine*: "From there, as Cosimo heard the parliament go into session, the sound of arms in the square and the peal of bells, he feared for his life." Puccio Pucci came to the rescue by oiling the hands of Bernardo Guadagni with a thousand ducats, thereby assuring that a ten-year sentence of exile in Padua be imposed instead. The following year, Cosimo was already back in Florence, and thus began the reign of the Medici, which would continue more or less uninterrupted for some three centuries. It would also mark the start of a new period for the palazzo. From then on, it would undergo continuous work as it was enlarged and embellished, starting with the Sala dell'Udienza. As of 1441, it became the Council Room for the Duecento, two hundred citizens who decided which wars would be undertaken,

90

which alliances entered into, and how the army would be organized and the city lands divided up.

In the same year of 1441, the palace also witnessed a grim event. Knowing full well that he was acting for the Medici, the gonfalonier Bartolomeo Orlandini summoned Baldaccio d'Anghiari, the captain of the army, and ordered him to be killed and thrown down from the tower. Francesco di Tommaso, a noted prior, commented that all the people were very happy and praised the event so that the Council finally acknowledged that a "perfect deed had been done." Needless to say,

the inquiry came to nothing and was shelved because the persons implicated were "above suspicion." Clearly the power of the Medici was already established.

Expansion on the palace continued apace until 1454 with Michelozzo, the Medici's favorite architect. Nine windows were put in, the galleries were restored, the courtyard was laid out, and a bronze pinnacle was placed atop the tower. Between 1475 and 1480, Benedetto and Giuliano da Maiano took over the work. The great hall on the second floor was divided into the Gigli and Udienza rooms. The ceiling in the latter was decorated with octagonal gilded intarsio panels. There were also other decorative works and reliefs, including the Door of Justice, and a marble statue holding a globe in one hand and a sword and golden scales in the other; these would, one day, mysteriously disappear. All the halls were finely furnished and frescoed. Verrocchio sculpted his *David* which was duly placed at the top of the staircase; Domenico Ghirlandaio executed the frescoes for the Sala dei Gigli and the other frescoes were done by Pollaiuolo and Botticelli. All of these, however, were destined to disappear.

The restored palace would see more bloodshed on Sunday, 26 April 1478 with the Pazzi conspiracy. Lorenzo and Giuliano de' Medici came under attack at S. Maria del Fiore, while Archbishop Salviati, his brother Jacopo, and Jacopo Bracciolini, together with a group of followers from Perugia, entered the palace. The archbishop told the gonfalonier Cesare Petrucci that he was bringing a message from the pope. Seeing such a large number of people, Petrucci grew suspicious and, guessing rightly that the archbishop was attempting to take the palace, called out loudly for the priors. Realizing he was raising the alarm, the priors took up arms, flew upon the conspirators and stopped them. Justice was summary: the three were hung on the spot and the survivors were hurled out of the windows. When Jacopo de' Pazzi arrived on horseback with a hundred armed men, the priors rained stones down on them, forcing them to flee. Revenge did not end there. The people hunted down the other members of the Pazzi family who had taken part in the attempted coup. Francesco was dragged from his house; Giovanni was discovered in a convent and Giovanni di Piero was

*Opposite, decorative details in the Studiolo di Francesco I, with allegories relating to alchemy. The walls are fully taken up with cupboards, the doors of which are painted by Vasari.*

*A corner of the Sala di Clemente VII, a room entirely decorated with scenes from the life of this pope. In particular, the famous fresco showing* The Siege of Florence of 1530 *and two ceiling ovates.*

stopped as he tried to take refuge in S. Croce, dressed as a woman. All three were hanged from the windows of the palace. The following day, the elderly Jacopo was caught up with on the hills while Antonio da Volterra and the priest Stefano, who had assaulted the Medici in the church, were also taken. They too were hanged. All told, including those hanged at the palace or killed in the streets, about one hundred people died.

After order had been reestablished in the palace, Lorenzo the Magnificent ruled over the city's magistrates until Girolamo Savonarola, the prior of S. Marco, spoke out in no uncertain terms denouncing the dissolute habits of the lay and clerical Florentines. He foretold the coming of an avenger from across the Alps (who would take the form of Charles VIII) and the death of Lorenzo. When this latter occurred, his son Piero de' Medici, could not hold onto power and fled for his life. Once again, the republic ruled itself while the people looked to Savonarola as he led the Piagnoni, his wailing followers. He started to influence political life from the palace, taking part in the constitutional debate and the reform of the state into a council of 1000 citizens with unblemished reputations, of whom 500 would suffice to elect 2,200 equally unblemished citizens.

A new hall in the palace was required and would be the Sala Grande, designed in 1496 by Simone del Pollaiuolo, called il Cronaca and a devoted follower of Savonarola. It was 52 meters long and 22 meters wide and was the largest hall in the palace when the council met there for the first time on 26 April to set up the Signoria, or ruling body. The monks of S. Marco celebrated the mass. On 20 August of the same year, Savonarola preached to the gathered magistrates and leading citizens regarding the upkeep of the new government. At Christmas, to save the city from papal armies, the monk proclaimed Jesus to be King of Florence.

On 8 April 1498, however, Savonarola entered the palace as a prisoner. His preaching had resulted in Pope Alexander VI accusing him of simony and excommunicating him. He also threatened to lay Florence under an interdict if it did not stop the monk preaching. The Signoria understood it was in their interest to heed the Pontifical State and proceeded to arrest Savonarola . He was tried on 19 April in the very Sala Grande that he had had built and where he had preached. With him were two monks, Domenico Buonvicini and Silvestro Maruffi. They were all sentenced to death on May 22 as heretics and schismatics. The sentence was carried out in the square in front of the palace the following day. The condemned men were first hanged and then burned on a pile of wood which set off gunpowder so that "in a few hours, amid explosions and rockets, they were burned," as Luca Landucci wrote in his *Diario*. The ashes were scattered in the Arno.

The 15th century closed with yet another bloodletting at the palace. On 1 October 1499, Paolo

*The Sala di Clemente VII, with wall frescoes illustrating episodes in the Siege of Florence of 1530 and a series of paintings relating to the life of the pope and his meetings with Francis I and Charles V; the ceiling of the room is divided into nine coffers, with intermediate ovates and rectangles, decorated with stucco ornament and figures representing other incidents in the life of Clement VII.*

*On the following pages, one side of the Sala dei Gigli, with frescoes by Ghirlandaio that divide the wall into three architectural elements with a classical flavor:* left, *Brutus, Scaevola and Camillus;* right, *Decius, Scipio and Cicero;* center, *Saint Zacharias between Saint Lawrence and Saint Stephen.*

BRVTVS          SCEVOLA          CAMILLVS

BRVTVS EGO ASSERTOR PATRIAE REGVMQ. FVGATOR
VRO MANVM SPRET          SCEVOLA FLAMMIS
HOSTE. ERO CAESO VICTRICIA SIGNA  CAMILLVS

EVGENIVS
DIACONVS

SVM NATO EXEMPLVM DECIVS·SVM VICTIMA ROME·
SCIPIO SVM·VICI HANNIBALEM·POENOSQ·SVBEGI·
SVM CICERO·TREMVIT NOSTRAS CATILINA SECVRES·

·DECIVS·    ·SCIPIO·    ·CICERO·

97

Vitelli, the captain of the army, was executed for betrayal during the war with Pisa. As for the people in the square waiting to watch the execution: "We were waiting for him to be thrown down from the palace but they didn't throw him. Instead they showed the people his head from the gallery windows, lit up by a torch, on the end of a stick."

During the time of the republic, the palace grew resplendent with art and was decorated and embellished in line with the city's prestige. Between 1503 and 1505, the two artists Leonardo da Vinci and Michelangelo started to work, in vain as it turned out, on frescoes on opposing walls of the Sala del Gran Concilio. There was a race to see who would finish first. The subjects chosen were respectively the *Battaglia di Anghiari* (Battle of Anghiari) and the *Battaglia di Cascina* (Battle of Cascina). It seems that the cartoons were put in place but the works were never finished and only copies by pupils have come down to us. Leonardo did in fact start painting but, instead of using the slow, traditional fresco technique, he used a new, faster experimental method of his own devising which he intended to dry using fire, thus beating his rival. However, the fire caused the colors to run down the wall, completely ruining the work. Michelangelo apparently also started his fresco, but he never finished it, possibly because he was also working on his *David* in front of the palace (where a copy now stands), and, in any case, he was called to Rome by Julius II to do other work. So the palace was the scene of one of the greatest failures in the history of art.

*Statue of* John the Baptist *in the Sala dei Gigli, placed on the trabeation of the portal by Benedetto and Giuliano da Maiano, flanked by putti candlesticks.*

In 1510, a new clock was installed on the tower. It was made by Lorenzo della Volpaia who was employed by the republic at a salary of eight lire, six soldi and eight denari plus two bushels of wheat a year. Recorded precisely in the city annals, it was the salvation of a man who, despite being brilliant for his times, ran the risk of not getting enough to eat.

The Medici returned to the palace in 1512, an event which was marked by the setting up of a guard of mercenary footmen at the great doors. The Sala del Gran Consiglio was made ready for them, and became, in effect, the Sala della Guardia. More happily, the chapel, which up until this time had been somewhat stark, underwent improvement. In 1514, Ridolfo da Ghirlandaio covered the walls and the vaulted ceiling with frescoes illustrating sacred texts and references to the good government of the city. On the altar there was a *Madonna col Bambino, Santa Elisabetta e San Giovanni* (Madonna and child with St. Elizabeth and St. John) by Mariano di Pescia, one of Ghirlandaio's students.

The year 1527 marked the final republican period and started with the second flight of the Medici. The palace once again became the focus of dreams of freedom. But it would have to be defended against

the designs of the emperor who was set on putting an end to Florence's delicate autonomy. In vain did the government turn to the Almighty for help, to Savonarola's Christ as the king of Florence; in vain did gonfalonies Niccolò Capponi have the words

*The Sala delle Carte Geografiche, with fifty-seven maps by Ignazio Danti and Stefano Bonsignori, the court cartographers; these decorate the outside of the movable panels by Dionigi Nigetti and show the then-known world. Center, the great globe. Top, the map of Italy.*

"Iesus Christus Rex Florentini Populi s.p. Decreto Electus" carved on the doors of the palace. In the Sala del Gran Consiglio, now rid of the Guards, two marble plaques were erected. This was in fulfillment of one of Savonarola's wishes. They were inscribed with two verses, the last lines of which warned citizens against preventing meetings. The plaques were solemnly unveiled on 10 June 1528. And the following year, the new gonfalonier Francesco Carducci had these words inscribed on the marble over the door of the Sala dell'Udienza: "Sol Iustitiae Christus Deus Noster Regnat in Aeternum." All to no avail. Charles V was not to be stopped by Christ the King or anyone else. The republic was ended once and for all as the Medici, under Duke Alessandro, retook the ancient palace from the priors. On 1 May 1532 Giovanfrancesco de' Nobili, the last gonfalonier of Florence, welcomed the new prince of the city through the great doors and handed power to him as the crowd in the square shouted "Palle! Palle!," referring to the balls on the Medici coat of arms, and "Duca! Duca!" as salvoes were fired into the air.

The palace would again change appearance as Alessandro saw fit to remove the great bell which had come to symbolize the republic: "So that we could no longer hear the sweet sound of liberty," commented Bernardo Davanzati, a merchant. The building would become the seat of the government's representatives; however, the duke had little interest in it as such, spending more time in his family's residence in the Via Larga until he was stabbed to death by his cousin Lorenzo in January 1537. Restoration fell to the new duke, Cosimo I, and the building's fortunes improved. From being merely the seat of the government, it also became the residence of the Lord of Florence. Three years after work to embellish the palace had started, he went to live there with his wife Eleonora of Toledo. Work would continue until his death, even though he moved to the Palazzo Pitti in 1565 leaving the palace to his son and successor Francesco.

Under the direction of Vasari, the building was divided up into parts, an operation which utterly changed its character from being a public edifice to being a noble home. Apartments on the main

*The Audience Room, where the priors administered justice, with frescoes depicting* The History of Furius Camillus, *painted by Francesco Salviati between 1543 and 1545. The coffered ceiling is by Battista del Tasso.*

reception floor were dedicated to the memory of outstanding Medici personalities: Leo X, the first Medici pope, Cosimo the Elder, Lorenzo the Magnificent, Cosimo I, son of the famous soldier of fortune Giovanni delle Bande Nere, and the second Medici pope, Clement VII. All the rooms had frescoes exalting the noble personages that had once occupied them.

On the second floor were the apartments of the Elementi, the elements, with their five rooms and two loggias decorated with symbolic paintings of the sun and the moon and the ducal virtues. Finally, there were Eleonora's apartments, including the Camera Verde (green room), which was finely decorated with Ghirlandaio grotesques, the duchess's study and chapel, as well as a suite of rooms for the court ladies in waiting. The podium was built in the Sala dei Cinquecento and, on its raised ceiling, the *Esaltazione di Cosimo* was painted, an apotheosis of his reign with scenes of his victories at Pisa and Siena painted on the walls. The whole was dominated by Michelangelo's *Vittoria* (Victory), which had been sculpted for Julius II in Rome but later given to Cosimo I. It symbolized the changeover of power and the complete disappearance of the priors of republican times.

The most important ceremony to take place in the restored palace was Francesco de' Medici and Joan of Austria's wedding in 1565. This was the occasion for elaborate decorations, especially in the courtyard where Tadda's fountain with its winged cherub by Verrocchio played. The columns were covered with stucco decorative motifs, depicting all the cities under Hapsburg rule, and leaves while grotesques covered the vault. The other grandiose work carried out for the wedding was the Corridoio which links the building to the Palazzo Pitti. This is a long gallery which starts in the Boboli Gardens, forms a bridge over Piazza Santa Felicita, passes through the church of the same name, forms another bridge over the Via de' Bardi and goes round the tower belonging to the Mannelli family who refused to let it go through their building. From there, it runs along the Ponte Vecchio and along Lungarno degli Archibusieri, flanking the river, from whence it goes into the

The Triumph of Camillus, *a fresco by Francesco Salviati on a wall in the Audience Room.*

*Right, double portrait of* Eleonora of Toledo, Wife of Cosimo I, with Her Son, Giovanni de' Medici, *by Agnolo Bronzino, painted c. 1544–45, now in the Uffizi.*

*Below, view of the Chapel of Eleonora of Toledo, frescoed between 1540 and 1546. The small door is surmounted by an arch in which the Trinity is depicted. The altarpiece is a replica of* Christ Taken Down from the Cross *by Agnolo Bronzino. At the sides, frescoes of* The Annunciation *and* David and the Eritrean Sybil, *painted c. 1560.*

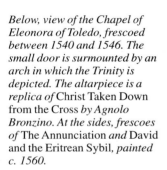

Uffizzi and ends up at the Palazzo Vecchio. More than anything else, the Corridoio was built so Cosimo could flee quickly in case of public rebellion into his palace; however, it was also a private place from where the comings and goings of the city's merchants and subjects could be watched unobserved. In 1866 the Corridoio was opened to the public, showing precious designs, prints and miniatures as well as the famous collection of self-portraits by European artists that Cardinal Leopoldo had initiated in the 17th century.

It was while Cosimo was at the Palazzo Pitti that a very special room would be added to the Palazzo Vecchio. This came about because of his son Francesco, who lived in the old palace with his wife. A keen alchemist, he had a study built on the main reception floor between 1570 and 1572. This little gem was where the young Medici carried out his experiments, surrounded by frescoes on art and nature and allegorical scenes which expressed his quests and his dreams. Windowless and lit only by the odd oil lamp, it is a sort of grotto of mysteries. It was decorated by Vasari and Vincenzo Borghini, the prior of the Ospedale degli Innocenti, working with

a team of painters and sculptors who executed the more than 40 works in this, Francesco's private museum and treasure house. It offered quite a temptation for a Frenchman called Michelagnolo (unrelated to the artist), who managed to steal some jewels from there in 1579, but who was caught and hanged for his pains.

The palace of the priors and the duke acquired its present name once and for all in 1587 when Grand Duke Francesco died. He was succeeded by his brother Ferdinando, who put aside his purple cardinal robes, married Cristina of Lorraine and went to live at the Palazzo Pitti. The old building regained some of its glory on 25 October 1587 when some members of the Senato de' Quarantotto and the Consiglio dei Duecento pledged their loyalty in the Sala Grande, and again, a few days later, in a ceremony of homage rendered to the duchess. Even though Ferdinando extended the palace to the rear, it was only used for ceremonial functions. The pomp and splendor became a thing of the past and the building would be at pains to maintain its dignity as time took its toll.

The name Vecchio stuck because, bit by bit, its works of art would be moved to the Uffizi Gallery.

Francesco's little study was completely destroyed, reduced to charcoal and was reconstructed with its original materials only in 1910. To some extent, the palazzo again became a focus of public life when the citizens celebrated the feast of St. John the Baptist. The Salone, which had once been used for court balls, played host to farmers and artisans and their wives during a three-day dancing festivity. The grand duke proffered wines and sweets and, at the end of the partying, sat in the square under a canopy to receive the homage of his subjects. Events when the palace was specially decorated became less regular. In 1607, a sumptuous banquet was offered by the Florentine aristocracy on the occasion of Cosimo II's wedding to Maria Maddalena of Austria. In 1615 a new bell was erected on the tower, and in 1667 there was the addition of a new clock made by Giorgio Lederle di Augusta.

The building went into increasing decline. In 1690, a fire destroyed 27 rooms, and with them were lost frescoes, manuscripts and relics forgotten there since the time of Cosimo I. The damage was estimated at approximately 120,000 scudi. And yet, even in the fire-scorched building, Ramadan Bassà,

*Passage through the Red Sea, a fresco by Bronzino in the Chapel of Eleonora of Toledo.*

the brother of the Bey of Tunisia, would find hospitality on 14 January 1694, when he stayed in the Elementi quarter for a week.

Glories were becoming a thing of the past, occurring only rarely and even then they lacked the special touch. On 7 March 1732, the last feast for the heir, Don Carlo of Lorraine, took place and fireworks were set off from the tower. On 12 July 1737, city representatives used the Salone to declare their loyalty to Francesco of Lorraine, the last official act performed by the duke which also honored the palace. The last works of art were removed and collections of arms and pottery were sold off. Courtly life meanwhile carried on at the Palazzo Pitti.

The restoration works commissioned by Ferdinand III in 1792 were somewhat summary, consisting of stone-colored plaster work around the tower and the galleries. The works carried out by the architect Giuseppe del Russo in 1809 were more noteworthy, in spite of some surrounding buildings being pulled down.

The palace again became the focus of city life in 1849, when the Tuscan parliament met there, and played a pivotal role ten years later, in 1859, when Tuscany was annexed by the kingdom of Italy. As the national capital from 1865 to 1870, Florence used the Palazzo Vecchio as its parliament building. The Salone dei Cinquecento became the Chamber of Deputies, while the Senate was housed in the Sala dei Duecento. The city hall began operating there in 1872. It was during this time that effective restoration work was carried out. This put the accent back on the civic function of the building and gave it back its original role as the city's municipal center. Some rooms have been maintained in their original splendor, and it is these which make the palazzo the most beautiful city hall in Italy.

*Above,* The Birth of Venus, *symbolizing* Water, *is one of the frescoes of the* Room of Elements, *the walls of which are entirely decorated with scenes from the life of Venus; top left, bust of a Roman emperor.*

*Opposite, a corner of the* Room of Elements, *with wall frescoes showing* Fire, *with Vulcan's forge, and* Water, *with the birth of Venus.*

# PALAZZO COMUNALE, PISTOIA

*The Palazzo Comunale, Pistoia on the Piazza del Duomo and, opposite, a detail of the facade, at the corner of the bridge that links it to the Cathedral.*

Civil conflict between opposing factions gave rise to this palazzo, which overlooks the Cathedral square and stands next to the building that was the residence of the *podestà*, or chief magistrate, and that, rebuilt, now houses the Court. The feuds of the Guelphs and the Ghibellines tore apart the free Municipality of Pistoia, one of the most ancient in Italy, with statutes dating from 1177; the fighting reached a climax in 1294, when the Florentine Giano della Bella was *podestà*, and the White Guelphs, who wanted complete independence for the Municipality, were victorious.

In this year construction of the *palatium communis* was begun on a site created by the demolition of properties that had belonged to the proscribed Ghibellines and Black Guelphs. The building work was was interrupted however by the return of the Black Guelphs and the Signoria of Castruccio Castracani, after which Pistoia became finally subject to the rule of Florence in 1399. Eventually, there was a period of peace and building began again, with considerable extensions added in 1348 under the direction of the Sienese Michele di Memmio.

It must have been at this time that the so-called "Moor's Head," fixed to a metal baton, was placed near the central window of the facade. This may be the head of Filippo Tedici, the traitor who in 1315 delivered the city to Castruccio. But it could possibly be Grandone de' Ghisilieri, who in 1114 led the forces of the Republic of Pisa in the conquest of the Balearic Islands, and the metal baton may have belonged to him.

Changes and alterations, based on no specific plan, were to be made over a long period, beginning with the interior tidying-up in the 15th century; and substantial work was done during the pontificates of the two Medicis, Leo X and Clement VII, as their coats of arms of 1513 and 1529 witness. But the changes carried out from the middle of the 16th century to the 17th century are more significant. For example, the fresco in the courtyard showing three horsemen: the one in the center is Cino da Pistoia (1270–1336), a *stil novo* poet also involved in politics, who, like Dante, trusted in the emperor Henry VII, and who lamented his death in the canzone *Da poi che la natura ha fine posto*. He was originally on the side of the Black Guelphs, whereas his son, Mino, was a Ghibelline supporter; he was exiled from 1303 to 1306, and when he returned to Pistoia with the Black Guelphs he acted for the Municipality in the office of assistant judge in civil proceedings.

The upper floor of the palazzo is especially impressive: it includes the Sala Maggiore, or Great Hall, with its carved and gilded wooden stalls made in 1536 by Giovanni Mati and his son, Bartolomeo; the frescoes of the Cappella di Sant'Agata, the work of Giuseppe Nasini; the Sala Ghibellina, now the Council Chamber, with the *Maestà* (Virgin in

*Opposite, top, detail of the exterior facade, a great mass of sandstone; bottom left, detail of the courtyard with its wide arches and, in the center, the bronze statue of 1953 by Marino Marini, Miracolo; right, an anonymous early 15th-century stone lion.*

*The courtyard of the palazzo seen from the second floor, with characteristic triple-mullioned windows and the bronze statue by Iorio Vivarelli, Herod, dating from 1971, on the right.*

Majesty) of Benozzo Gozzoli; and the Sala Guelfa, now the Mayor's Parlor, with Gimignani's *L'Ultima Cena* (Last Supper). And finally, on the second floor, are the Sala dei Donzelli with its fine coffered wood ceiling, and the Sala dei Priori, both now part of the Civic Museum, which the palazzo became in 1922. The establishment of this museum was a remarkable achievement, because, to its credit, the Municipality brought together works from the collections of religious institutions suppressed in the 18th and 19th centuries. The Museum was reorganized in 1956 and moved two years later to another building, but it returned here in 1982, with a rich documentation center, as a sign that the palazzo has an artistic purpose and is not limited to the carrying out of municipal business.

Three contemporary sculptures in the courtyard should also be mentioned: Marino Marini's *Miracolo*, Agenore Fabbri's *Pietà* and *Ercole* by Torio Vivarelli.

# PALAZZO PANNOCCHIESCHI D'ELCI, SIENA

This palazzo is, as it were, "at the starting gate"; from the windows that overlook the Campo you can enjoy the start of the Palio, the famous horse race, from a privileged position. It is perhaps more exciting than being on the course itself, because often a good position in the street below determines the outcome of the race. From the vantage point of this building you can enjoy a show within a show, and it is the ambition of both Sienese and foreigners to be invited there by the owners, the Counts Pannocchieschi d'Elci. Among recent famous visitors is the British prime minister, Tony Blair, who watched the Palio from there in August of 1999.

The palazzo's origins lie in the 13th century, when it was the property of the Alessi and already had the battlements of a fortified dwelling that were to remain a characteristic mark, an emblem even, of its architectural nobility. The anonymous architects of the Palazzo Pubblico are said to have taken it as a model for the building of the seat of government that was to dominate the Campo. That the Sienese authorities were involved with the Palazzo Alessi is proven by the fact that until 1291 the

*View of the Palazzo Pannocchieschi d'Elci, which dominates the Campo of Siena. The palazzo was the first to be built on the Campo, in 1180.*

because the Municipality had in the meantime built suitable accommodation in the Palazzo Pubblico. The Cerretani owned the palazzo until the end of the 18th century, the longest period it remained in the possession of the same family; though part of it was sold to Niccoluccio and Ugo Ricasoli in 1361, only to be bought back again 20 years later. The Cerretani gave the palazzo its history in this Terzo, or district, of the city, taking part in the life of Siena as the noblemen representing the Contrada della Selva, or "Forest District," and having the means to embellish the interior of the building at the height of the Renaissance, when almost all the palazzi on the Via di Città were being renovated.

In the early years of the 18th century the Cerretani sold part of the palazzo to the Cioni family, who passed it on to the aristocratic Pannocchieschi d'Elci, who became the owners of the whole building. However, it still belonged to the Cerretani, in the person of Bandinello de' Bandinelli Paparoni, when in 1798 a violent earthquake damaged the tower and demolished its two upper floors. The Cerretani paid for the rebuilding work, but only dealt with the exterior. The tower had its Guelph battlements restored and the walls were plastered, though only to give a false stone effect.

*Left, the drawing room known as the Passage Room. The two armchairs in the foreground are of Sienese make, in the imperial style. Above the door, decoration with drapery made by Agostino Fantastici.*

*Below, detail of the Yellow Room, decorated in 1899 for the wedding of Nello Pannocchieschi d'Elci to Marina Bindi Sergardi. The large portrait shows a member of the family who was ambassador to the court of Spain.*

tower was one of the seats of the Supreme Magistrate of the Signoria; part of the building was leased to the Commander of the Militia and other officials. Furthermore, prisoners were kept in the cellars and on the ground floor. The palazzo functioned as a prison for 40 years, and this use is still remembered today in the name of the Chiasso del Bargello (Prison Lane) to the left of the palazzo, between the Campo and the Via di Città.

In 1297 the palazzo was bought by Giacoppo Signieri Gallerani, who gained possession of the rooms occupied by municipal officials, although the governor reserved the right to use the ground floor as an armory and the cellars as a prison. Gallerani restored the palazzo and returned what had been used for military purposes to domestic use; but he did not come to live there. He gave it as a present to Musciatto Franzesi and his wife, the Contessa Rinaldini, who became its new owners. It was, however, an insecure tenancy; in 1308 the Municipality took possession of the whole palazzo because of certain tax debts. Franzesi's complaint to the Nine was successful and the building was given back to him on condition that he paid the debts. They were, in fact, paid by the Compagnia dei Peruzzi of Florence, which in 1309 became a successor in rights to the property, and it was to this Compagnia that the Municipality paid the rent for the armory and the prison.

The Franzesi returned to live there in 1318, but their financial position was not good, because they owed money to the Roman Curia. In 1326 they sold the palazzo to the Cerretani, who in 1330 were able to repossess the ground floor and the cellars,

*Detail of the great mirror
supported by a Louis XVI-style
console in the drawing room of
the palazzo.*

*Below, the Great Ballroom,
now a drawing room for
receiving guests. Between the
two gray sofas, a table with
some vases.*

The Pannocchieschi d'Elci, who had acquired the whole palazzo at the end of the 18th century, completely rebuilt the interior from 1814 onwards. They were an ancient Sienese family of aristocratic lineage, originating from Volerra, and could boast among their ancestors famous cardinals such as Scipione (c. 1600–70), Apostolic Nuncio to Vienna, Raniero (1670–1761), Apostolic Nuncio to Paris, and Francesco (1707–87), all three buried in the family chapel in S. Sabina in Rome. The most famous ancestor though would be Nello, Count of Petra, Captain General to the *Guelph* League and a contemporary of Dante, who in his *Divina Commedia* recounts the gruesome story of how Nello had his wife, Pia dei Tolomei, killed.

But in this palazzo aristocratic pride was expressed in the splendor of the rooms. Under the direction of the architect Agostino Fantastici the staircase was renewed, as were the bedroom, which acquired a colonnaded alcove, as well as the doorways, and the elegant double-doors of the *piano nobile* were installed. The palazzo was brilliant with the magnificence of both its furnishings and the events that took place there; in the middle of the 19th century the Salotto Rosso, or Red Drawing

*The great family tree, showing the 36 castles of Alta Maremma that belonged to the Pannocchieschi d'Elci family.*

*The Dining Room, richly ornamented with Ginori plates of 1756, decorated with enamel and Murano glass.*

113

*The Red Drawing Room, which was decorated in 1866 for the marriage of Achille Pannocchieschi d'Elci to Elena Pucci Sansedoni. The ceiling (detail, opposite page) is entirely covered with frescoes of the family coats of arms of the two spouses.*

Room was first used for the celebrated wedding of Achille d'Elci and Elena Pucci Sansedoni; in 1899 the Camera Gialla, or Yellow Room was also inaugurated at a wedding, that of Emanuello d'Elci and Marina Bindi Sergardi, when the century was brought to a close in a blaze of aristocratic splendor.

The palazzo also houses the d'Elci Archive, which is very important for investigations of the history of the family and the other families that succeeded it as owners, up to the Pannocchieschi d'Elci who still live there today in the person of the Contessa Cesarina, with her two sons, Andrea and Ranieri, and Ranieri's wife, Maria Eleanora Guasconi di Villamena.

116

*Left, details of the ceiling fresco of the Red Room.*

*Below, the Chapel of the Palazzo, with an 18th-century enamel and silver altar frontal attributed to Valadier.*

117

# PALAZZO DELLA FRATERNITA DEI LAICI, AREZZO

*The facade of the Palazzo della Fraternita dei Laici, Arezzo, with, on the left, the Palazzo del Tribunale.*

The Fraternita existed before the palazzo was built. It was endowed in 1262, for the purposes of Christian charity, by a group of lay people, advised by the Dominicans. A year earlier the bishop, Guglielmo degli Ubertini, had approved its incorporation as the Fraternita di Santa Maria della Misericordia, a name which well expressed the aims of the confraternity, which were to help the sick, the poor, and the needy. Its intricate calligraphic emblem consisted of an M for Mary and for Misericordia (Mercy), and an F for Fraternita.

No building was considered at the time, because the charitable activity consisted in going round the city begging, and then passing the collection on to those in need. Twice a week this was the task of the rectors of the Fraternita, who, as an expression of the solidarity of the city, were elected to represent the various districts of Arezzo; they carried the "tefanìa," a wooden container holding the bread they gave out, and a shoulder bag for the money they collected.

However, charitable citizens of Arezzo began to give donations and leave bequests, and it was decided that not only was there no longer any need to make collections in the streets, but really an administrative building was necessary in order to manage the property and invest the money. An office for the rectors, a records office, and a food store were required; and thus came about the idea of the palazzo.

It was planned in 1363, the centenary year of the confraternity, and a start was made with the purchase of municipal land on the Piazza Grande, which at that time was much larger than it is now. At the top it was marked out by the Palazzi del Comune and del Popolo, and at the bottom by the Hospital of Santa Maria de Platea and by the Petrone, a sort of "column of infamy," still in existence, though the present column is a copy of the original. Here criminals were put in the pillory and public proclamations were made. This piazza, the center of political and commercial life, where markets, tournaments, and jousts took place, seemed the best site for the quarters of the Fraternita, given the institution's popular character; the citizens of Arezzo must have felt closely associated with it, to the point of considering themselves all members, at once supporters and beneficiaries, should the need arise. It was a sort of foster-mother to them all. After all, did it not hold the city's Register of Deaths and Baptisms?

Building work started in 1375, and it was then that the work of Niccolò di Francesco and Baldino

*One end of the Palazzo Tribunale, which overlooks the Piazza Grande, with the apse of the parish church on the left.*

119

di Cino, two Florentine stone-carvers, began to appear on the facades; but it was interrupted, because between 1380 and 1384 Arezzo was sacked three times during the struggle for power of the aristocratic Guelph and Ghibelline families. Finally it lost its independence. Naturally the Fraternita suffered the consequences of a sacking such as that by Alberico da Barbiano and his plunderers on the night of 17/18 November 1381, which is described by the chronicler Giovanni Sercambi: *The whole city of Arezzo was looted and many Ghibellines were taken prisoner, and all the women were taken, both Guelphs and Ghibellines, in such numbers it was great pity, and they were disgraced... And the city was so treated that whoever should have seen it could not have forborne to pity them; to see so many gentlewomen and maidens and nuns put to shame and many becoming public whores, the children dying of hunger and for hunger eating the putrid offal of horses, even uncooked.*

It is probable that the Fraternita found it had no longer the money that had enabled it to set up an administrative organization and contemplate the building of a palazzo. The facade came to a stop at the first cornice above the arches, and, because of lack of funds, work did not continue after 1384. Spinelli's painting of the *Pietà* on the lunette of the porch in 1395 was an isolated episode; it was only in 1433, when, clearly, the Fraternita had managed to rearrange its finances, that building of the walls started again. The gifts of Lazzaro di Giovanni di Feo Bracci, known as "Lazzaro the Rich," were a godsend to the Fraternita; they enabled it to call in Bernardo Rossellino to continue the facade in a Renaissance style that fits admirably with the Gothic first floor.

When the bas-relief of the *Madonna col Bambino* (Madonna and Child), flanked by the kneeling Saints Lorentino and Pergentino, arrived on 30 June 1434 as decoration for the facade, it was an occasion for great celebrations, with the whole population crowding into the Piazza Grande to sing and dance. In 1460 a magnificent gallery was added, made by compatriots of Rossellino, Giuliano and Algozzo from Settignano; the palazzo now looked finished, but in fact it was still without its crowning feature.

Another hundred years were to pass before gifts from Francesco and Jacopo Viviani, Mariotto Cofani, and Angiolo Gambiglioni made possible the building of the vaulted campanile. It was designed by Vasari, and Felice da Fossato made its clock in 1552. The whole operation is surrounded with legend and mystery. Tradition has it that the maker went blind after he had finished the clock, because it was fated he should not make any others similar. Moreover, the face is marked out with a strange image based on the Ptolemaic system. At the center is an unfilled circle representing the earth, around which revolves a black and white circle, representing the moon, and a small golden

circle, the sun, revolves around both of them; under them revolves a metal disk marked with 29 numbers relating to the days of the lunar month, a mechanism that tends to get stuck, perhaps more so today than at the time it was made.

The palazzo was finally completed and in it the operations of the Fraternita went forward at full pace. It managed to carry on with the help of a succession of legacies made in the 16th and 17th

centuries, including those of the artist Giorgio Vasari and the scientist and poet Francesco Redi, and in the 18th century it received bequests from Benedetto and Roberto Sabatini, Vittorio Fossombroni, Donato Lombardi, Pietro Onesti, and Giuseppe Ninci. The Fraternita had huge assets that were administered by eight rectors, members of aristocratic Arezzo families. Wearing long black cloaks, they sat in the Sala Maggiore, the Great Hall, under the austere wooden ceiling, or heard petitions from citizens in the Sala delle Udienze (Audience Room) that was decorated with Parri di Spinello's fine fresco, the *Madonna della Misericordia*.

The rectors had the duty of carrying out the terms of benefactors' bequests, which, according to the report of a bishop who was the Fraternita's papal visitor, numbered 560 in 1583. They managed an annual income of 300 gold scudi and 10,000

*The west side of the Piazza Grande of Arezzo, on which stand, from the left, the apse of the parish church, the Palazzo del Tribunale, and the Palazzo della Fraternita, with its fine portal by Balduccio di Cino and Niccolò di Francesco, between two Gothic single windows.*

*Detail of the facade of the Palazzo della Fraternita dei Laici; note the lunette above the main portal, with a Pietà of 1395 by Spinello Aretino, and, above this, the central bas-relief in the mixtilinear cornice showing a Virgin with Child. At the side, in the niches, are statues of Saint Donatus and the Blessed Gregory by Bernardo Rossellino.*

bushels of grain, all of which had to be accounted for with the greatest transparency in a monthly calendar. The money was invested in housing for the poor, care of the sick, burial of the dead, and the restoration of churches. However, the Fraternita was also involved in public building work, such as the Palazzo delle Logge, designed by Vasari and sited at one corner of the Fraternita. They also sponsored educational initiatives, such as the 14 university scholarships for the young of Arezzo, and works like the 18th-century building of the muni-

cipal cemetery, the city's water distribution system dating from the late 19th century, and the Ninci orphanage. Of course, they also maintained their own palazzo, which in 1780 was enriched by a magnificent staircase designed by Angiolo Lorenzo de' Giudici, a native of Arezzo.

However, in 1786 came the first sign of crisis: the Grand Duke Leopoldo I ordered the Fraternita to lease the palazzo for use as a Civil Court, and the confraternity had to move its offices to the Palazzo Comunale, leaving behind only the Library and the

*The Madonna of Mercy, a fresco by Parri di Spinello in the Audience Room.*

Museum, two institutions that, because of their invaluable documentation of the culture and history of Arezzo, were to be the Fraternita's most lasting legacy.

The Fraternita carried on as usual and financed the restoration work which the palazzo was beginning to need. It still had money available: in 1882, an income of 80,000 lire. Subsequently, however, it no longer had a purpose, losing its historic function when the municipal authority and the state set up other systems that replaced its *raison d'être*.

The palazzo went into slow decline, its frescoes peeling from the walls, but it was later rescued, to contribute the harmony of its lines to one of the most beautiful squares in Italy.

# PALAZZO MEDICI-RICCARDI, FLORENCE

*Palazzo Medici-Riccardi, on the corner of the Via Cavour and the Via de' Gori, with the Medici arms on the corner and the arches of the enclosed loggia, with windows by Michelangelo. Right, detail of a twin-mullioned window on the south side of the courtyard.*

Cosimo the Elder (1429–64) wanted to build a palazzo which would not only serve as a home for his family but which would also represent the great power he enjoyed as a rich merchant who, while being in a position to influence public officials, was nevertheless a private citizen. Not an extravaganza then. Brunelleschi had other ideas, though, and

presented an ambitious project. This Cosimo considered too pompous and immediately rejected, "more to dispel envy than for its cost," because it could have made his rivals think that he was intending to take over direct control of the city's administration.

Michelozzo came up with a more sober design: an elegant building with a balanced, measured external aspect but where the interior details reflected the owner's every desire. It was approved, and work started in early 1444. The building that went up was like a cube and had ten windows overlooking the Via Larga. There was also a loggia to soften the powerful lines of the rusticated facade rising to the splendid cornice. In contrast to the

*The west wing of the courtyard of the Palazzo Medici-Riccardi, with back view of the 16th-century statue* Orpheus *by Baccio Bandinelli, situated in the center of the courtyard.*

On the following pages, the courtyard of the Palazzo Medici-Riccardi, showing the magnificence of the arcades and decoration by Michelozzo. On the first floor, the courtyard portico has Corinthian columns, and on the third floor there is a loggia with Ionic columns. The graffiti are the work of Maso di Bartolomeo and the medallions on the architrave above the arches are attributed to Bertoldo. On the right, the statue of Orpheus by Bandinelli, behind which is the entrance to the garden.

125

*Opposite, the shield with the Medici arms and the yoked-oxen device of Leo X by Benedetto da Rovezzano, on the marble base, of Bandinelli's Orpheus.*

*Details of decoration of the porticoes of the palazzo courtyard.*

somewhat severe exterior was the large, elegant internal courtyard affording light and air to the many rooms giving on to it. On the ground floor were the loggia and the rooms where business was carried out; a monumental stairway led up to the fine reception areas and the apartments of the nobleman himself. The decoration and furnishings of the rooms were designed to amaze and delight the eye, with works of art, precious stones, and

arms. Above were the bedrooms, minor apartments, and service areas.

The jewel, though, was the marvelous chapel. It was decorated in 1459 with frescoes of *L'Adorazione dei Magi* (The Adoration of the Magi) by Benozzo Gozzoli. The theme would become emblematic of the Medici family as members of the confraternity of the Magi, a Florentine religious association which was also open to humanists, and of which Cosimo the

Elder, and later his son Piero the Gouty and his grandson Lorenzo the Magnificent, would be presidents. But more especially, the frescoes were a hymn to the family, featuring, as they did, a courtly story set in the Tuscan landscape. They illustrate the three ages of man, with horsemen dressed in all their finery, some of whom were identified by André Chastel as famous individuals: *The oldest man is the patriarch of Constantinople who died in Florence after the famous council of 1439, while the melancholic man is the emperor John VIII who had signed a treaty for help against the Ottomans on that occasion… The painter included a Florentine Magus who was wearing the same costume he had worn for the oriental festivity held at the Piazza della Signoria in 1459: it was Lorenzo, wearing the same Turkish-style turban that can be seen on the Paleologue's head.*

In 1459, the palazzo began to host official functions, starting with the visit of Galeazzo Maria

Sforza, the oldest son of the duke of Milan, who was passing through Florence with Pope Pius II. The pope was on his way back from Mantua where he had called a congress of Christian princes in the vain hope of getting them to start a crusade. Galeazzo was full of admiration for the celebrations and wrote to his father telling him of his delight at the ball held in the Piazza S. Croce and the hunt for wild animals in the Piazza della Signoria. What impressed him most, though, was the splendid display of works of art that the Medici had in their noble home.

Less auspicious times were in store for the fine home and its master. They came in the shape of family misfortunes. In the same year of 1459, Cosimo's dearly beloved grandchild, the 3-year-old Cosimino, died; his eldest son, Piero, continued to be ill with gout, leaving little hope for a healthy successor while, hardest of all, in 1463, his second

*General view, from the south, of the enclosed garden of the palazzo, to a design by Michelozzo.*

son, Giovanni, upon whom Cosimo had pinned his hopes, also died. Greatly saddened, Cosimo wandered around the palazzo he had built so lovingly and which he now found: "too big for such a small family." The "father of the nation" died the following year, "lamented by his friends and enemies," as the words of Machiavelli engraved on the tomb in S. Lorenzo would read. Piero was not up to the challenge left him and his rivals lost little time in raising their sights.

One day in August 1466, Piero was nearly ambushed along his route as he returned, pain-ridden and litter-borne, from his country home at Careggi. It was only the quick thinking of his son Lorenzo that saved the day. The youth, who was at the head of the riding party, realized the danger they were in. He told the would-be attackers that his father was in the rearguard but managed to get word to him to take a different route and give them the slip while he, Lorenzo, sped home. The palazzo was quickly transformed into a stronghold and the youth set groups of armed men at the great doors, inside the courtyard, at the ready for the ambushers who soon arrived after failing to locate Piero.

The families that had ordered the attack, including the Pitti, went even further and turned to the gonfalonier Soderini for help to outwit the Medici; however, they would not have their way, for the common people had gathered around the parliament, cheering for Piero who was then authorized to lead the city for ten years. The Medici reacted with singular moderation. None of the death sentences proclaimed by the Signoria was carried out, resulting in the Medici gaining moral points from their humanitarian gesture.

The wedding day of Lorenzo to Clarice Orsini fell on 4 June 1469, and there were huge festivities at the palazzo which was overflowing with guests, including the important families of Florence. Outside, on the Via Larga, food and wine were provided for the populace for three days. Five thousand pounds of sweetmeats alone were consumed. In the palazzo gardens a play was performed; the allegory of a battle took place and carts carrying flowers and gifts for the people were pulled through the city. It was all aimed at paving the way for Lorenzo's path to personal power in the future.

Notwithstanding all this, tragedy would again strike the palazzo as Piero's health spiraled downwards. He passed his final months in terrible pain which neither sulfur baths nor fumigations could relieve. And yet, even from his sickbed, he still had occasional bursts of energy, such as when he summoned to his bedside some of his supporters who had become emboldened by the Medici success, in order to rebuke them for taking advantage of the citizens of Florence, abusing them and causing damage, and he threatened to recall the exiled enemy families to keep them in line. This act came with the fading of his strength. He died in the palazzo on 2 December 1469.

Gladder times would return, though. On 13 March 1471, Galeazzo Maria Sforza returned to Florence with his wife, Bona of Savoy, who possessed a magnificent wardrobe with exquisitely embroidered garments of cloth of gold and silver, "fit for the hospitality offered at the luxurious palazzo with its wealth of art treasures." Sforza, who had already seen the internal decoration of the palazzo, was amazed at how it had flourished over the last 12 years as a result of Lorenzo's attentions. As Scipione Ammirato recalled: *Greatly did he admire the many pictures painted by the best masters, as he himself was inclined much towards painting, and said that he had seen more in the Palazzo Medici than in the whole of Italy; and so with drawings, with statues and other works in marble, both modern works as well as ancient, of medals and jewels, books, and other singular and highly prized things.*

*Detail of the fountain in the garden, with a statue of Hercules.*

*On the preceding pages, view of the Salon of Charles VIII and corner of the "painted retreat" on the second floor of the Palazzo Medici-Riccardi.*

*Right and below, details of the reading room of the Biblioteca Riccardiana with shelving decorated with gilt stucco. The vaulted ceiling by Luca Giordano shows* The Allegory of Divine Wisdom.

The palazzo also became a meeting place for intellectuals who gathered around Lorenzo. He was learning about humanism through literature and art, and he himself would write verses extolling the need to be happy today for tomorrow might never come. There were also painters who visited such as Benozzo Gozzoli, Sandro Botticelli, Andrea del Verrocchio, and Domenico Ghirlandaio, poets like Angelo Poliziano and Luigi Pulci, and philosphers such as Marsilio Ficino and Giovanni Pico della Mirandola. Stories competed with each other, poetry was read, and there were courtly games; plays were performed in the torch-lit gardens and there was joyous music. It was all a hymn to fleeting life caught on the wing.

The noble residence thronged to the sound of the children born to Lorenzo and Clarice: the two first boys were Piero, born in 1472, and Giovanni, born in 1475. These were followed by three girls, Lucrezia, born in 1470, Maddalena in 1473, and Lucia in 1477. Yet two more children would be born, in 1478 a boy, called Giuliano, and another girl, called Contessina. In that year, however, the Pazzi attacked again, and on 26 April Lorenzo was wounded in church and carried by Poliziano back to his palazzo; his brother Gialiano was killed. That day signaled the moment when Lorenzo started his rise to power as the Magnificent: the crowd gathered in front of his palazzo to hear news of his well-being and cheered him wildly when he addressed them, exhorting them to remain calm. He became what Giovanni Cambi later described slyly in his *Delizie*

*degli eruditi toscani*, as more of a tyrant than a master with a stick.

For a while, until the end of 1479, Lorenzo lived without his wife and children in the palazzo, having moved them to Pistoia for safety a few days after the Pazzi conspiracy. On their return to Florence, they went to live in the villa at Cafaggiolo. The palazzo became increasingly connected with official business and, as such, hosted the festivities held in honor of his second son, Giovanni, when he became a cardinal on the 9 March 1492, when he was only 17 years old.

The death of Lorenzo the Magnificent one month later started a period of crisis at the palazzo. Piero, his firstborn son and successor, fell victim to the violent prophesies of Savonarola and ended up appearing as a traitor when the French king Charles VIII arrived on 17 November 1494. Piero was forced to flee Florence and the palazzo was sacked. Many works of art were lost, while pieces of furniture and precious articles were auctioned off publicly. The great house was already stripped when the French king arrived and took charge for the ten stormy days during which the peace negotiations took place. When the king did not receive the money he had demanded, he threatened to "sound my trumpets!" – only to be answered by Pier Capponi, the representative of the Republic, announcing: "and we shall ring our bells!" as he tore up the copy of the treaty and stormed off down the stairs. The king called him back, however, and with a smile as Jacopo Nardi noted in his *Istorie*,

*The Gallery of the Palazzo Medici Riccardi, with ceiling frescoed by Luca Giordano between 1682 and 1685, showing the* Apotheosis of the Medici*, the walls decorated with stucco and mirrors.*

said: "Ah Ciappon, Ciappon, you are a naughty Ciappon," and so, happily, peace was made.

When the Medici returned to Florence in 1512, they took repossession of the palazzo and sent out an ordinance to try to get back the lost furnishings and works of art, and indeed "many things" did return to the house, as Luca Landucci noted somewhat vaguely in his *Diario*. One year later, the family and the palazzo were greatly honored by the election to the papacy of Giovanni de' Medici, who took the name of Leo X. On 11 March 1513, Scipione Ammirato noted, the new pope's brother

Giuliano and his nephew Lorenzo "threw all sorts of clothes and silver and gold coins out of the palazzo windows to the clapping crowd below."

To reaffirm the family's importance, when the pope visited Florence on 30 November 1515 he stayed in the palazzo where he had been born, thus making sure that it once again became the symbol of Medici power, this time in the person of his nephew Lorenzo. He also chose a lady of high birth for Lorenzo to marry. This was the French noblewoman Madeleine de la Tour d'Auvergne. The wedding was celebrated in France in 1518. Soon

*Detail of the large ceiling fresco of the Gallery, showing* The Apotheosis of the Medici.

afterwards, the honeymoon couple went to live in the noble Florentine residence where Catherine, the last descendant of Cosimo the Elder, and the future queen of France, would be born on 13 April 1519.

In that same year though the young couple died and Leo X delegated the running of the palazzo to his cousin Giulio, a cardinal. When he too became pope in 1523, taking the name of Clement VII, the job passed to Cardinal Silvio Passerini, because the remaining grandchildren of Lorenzo the Magnificent, Ippolito, aged 14 and Alessandro aged 12,

were too young. The new Republic was declared in 1527 and the Medici again had to leave their palazzo, but not for long: in 1531, the emperor Charles V relegated power yet again to the Medici and Alessandro was elected head of the state and of the kingdom which was in truth only a duchy. To lend prestige to the new dynasty, the emperor had him marry his natural daughter Margarita, thus linking the Medici to the Hapsburgs.

Margarita was only 12 at her meeting with the duke when she visited Florence on 16 April 1532. The young girl was received with due honors at the

EN PICTVRA DOCET VARYS ANIMATA FIGVRIS
QVOD VIRTVS HOMINES ASSERIT VNA
DEOS

Medici palazzo and much feasting and merry-making was enjoyed on the Via Larga, including Saracen jousting. This was followed by an official visit by Charles V, on 26 April 1536, and gave occasion to a procession which wended its way round the city streets under artificial arches all the way to the Medici palazzo where the emperor stayed for a week, the duration of the festivities in his honor. Over the door a banner was affixed which read: "Ave Magne Hospes Auguste."

Finally, the wedding took place in Naples on 31 May 1536; however, the celebrations were held in Florence. A grand banquet was organized for the Florentine nobles in the palazzo; there were balls and in the evening there was a performance of *L'Aridiosa*, a play by Lorenzino de' Medici, Alessandro's cousin.

It was this cousin who would put an end to the palazzo's first ducal family. The following January, Lorenzino betrayed Alessandro, murdering him in his own house beside the palazzo. There were fears for the duchy, but it turned out to be business as usual with the rise to power of Cosimo di Giovanni, who was elected as the new duke and immediately

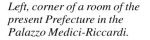
*Opposite,* Minerva Handing a Key and a Tool to Invention and Skill, *detail of Luca Giordano's fresco in the Gallery.*

*Left, corner of a room of the present Prefecture in the Palazzo Medici-Riccardi.*

*On the following pages, one side of the Chapel of the Magi, with a cycle of frescoes painted by Benozzo Gozzoli between 1459 and 1461. Center,* The Procession of the Magi *and, left, a detail of* The Procession of the Young King.

*Detail of* The Procession of the Moorish King, *the Byzantine emperor John VIII Paleologus, on the back wall of the Chapel of the Magi.*

144

took up residence in the palazzo. Lorenzino fled to Venice and his house was knocked down. Margarita left Florence for Rome where she was remarried, this time to Ottavio Farnese, having refused to become the wife of the new duke. He, in turn, took as wife Eleonora of Toledo, the daughter of Don Pedro, the vice-king of Naples; so one way and another Cosimo got an equally noble wife.

This wedding was yet another celebration unparalleled for pomp and splendor and the palazzo was adorned as it had never been before that particular day, 6 July 1539. The nuptial banquet held in the garden was surrounded by scenes featuring the exploits of the Medici family and the wedding ceremony itself. The feasting was repeated again in the garden three days later with another group of guests and was followed by a musical entertainment and a performance of Antonio Landi's play, *Il Commodo*. The grand finale was a mythological ballet which took the form of a bacchanal in which everyone participated.

It was the last festive event to be organized by a Medici in the palazzo, because in 1540 Cosimo took

*Opposite,* The Procession of the Old King, *on the left wall of the Chapel of the Magi, and, left, a detail of the fresco.*

*Below, members of the Medici family and other Florentines saluting the passing of* The Procession of the Old King, *in a detail from the said fresco.*

up residence in the Palazzo Vecchio, so as to underline his absolute power more visibly. From then on, lesser personalities from the minor branches of the family lived in the palazzo and it consequently lost a little of its splendor. These included Pietro di Cosimo I (1554–1604) and the two cardinals Ferdinando and Carlo. Finally, in March 1659, Grand Duke Ferdinando II decided to sell the building to the marquis Gabriello Riccardi for 40,000 scudi.

The Riccardi family, who originally came from Germany, had lived in Florence since the 14th century. As tailors and textile merchants they had lived in relative obscurity, not entering the limelight until they had the fortune to come into the good graces of the Medici. A certain Francesco became senator in 1569 while a Cosimo was appointed governor of Leghorn in 1648 by Ferdinando II. The latter also raised the family to the nobility by bestowing the title of marquis of Chienna, Rivalto, and Montevaso upon it. The ennobling process obviously had something to do with the sale of the house for, that way, it would remain inhabited by an aristocratic family.

The Riccardi were very wealthy and as such felt that the palazzo should be fitted out to suit the pomp and circumstance they knew was their due. They embarked on a series of works which in the end cost them three times what the Medici had spent on the building itself. In particular, the facade was increased to twice its size, taking in the block where Lorenzino's house had stood, and stretching all the way down the Via Larga, the present-day Via Cavour. They extended the back of the building on to the present-day Via Ginori, in every case following the plans drawn up by the architects Giovanni Battista Foggini and Pier Maria Baldi. Part of the inside was also modified, with connecting stairs and restoration work carried out inside the rooms. A vast gallery frescoed by Luca Giordano was opened, which would become in effect a museum for gem stones and bronzes. A library also came into being and its ceiling was painted by Giordano.

The library collection was primarily made up of manuscripts, incunabula (books printed prior to 1501), and prints. Over the next 50 years, it would expand into several other rooms to become the Biblioteca Riccardiana, open for consultation by scholars and organized by the passionate book lover of the family, Gabriello (1705–98), who even contrived a system of book lending.

The sumptuous Riccardi festivities and salons were always open to the Medici who came as guests of honor. Thus Cosimo III was invited to a ball on 7 February 1677. In January 1689, the Riccardi were honored to hold a wedding reception for Ferdinando, son of Cosimo III, and his bride Violante Beatrice of Bavaria. The day was chosen for the frescoes by Luca Giordano to have their official showing and they were greatly admired by the illustrious guests. It was probably then that the allegorical *Glorificazione dei Medici* went down in history.

148

*Opposite,* The Young King, *an idealized portrait of Lorenzo the Magnificent, who was 20 when the fresco was painted.*

*The archers in* The Procession of the Old King.

Angels in Adoration, *fresco by Benozzo Gozzoli on the left wall of the apse of the Chapel of the Magi.*

Each and every occasion provided an excuse for the Riccardi family to organize feasts for the sheer pleasure of showing off their wealth. In March 1709, the king of Denmark and Norway, Frederick IV, was honored during a visit to Florence by a nighttime reception at the palazzo where the decorations were simply dazzling, 28 of the rooms being decorated with tapestries and damask hangings. As Giovanni Battista Casotti noted in his *Diario*, 80 barrels of candied fruit jams were eaten during the feast, while the populace in the streets were given an abundance of sugared almonds, chocolate, and coffee.

of Hapsburg and Maria Beatrice d'Este visited Florence, and to these the grand duke, his wife Marie Louise of Bourbon, and their son Francesco were naturally invited. The party spread over 32 rooms, two of which were reserved for dancing and boasted a 20-piece orchestra. Four thousand people took part and it went on until dawn.

Bit by bit the Riccardi family used up their entire fortune and were forced to sell the palazzo in 1810. Their precious collections, including the library, were put up for auction. The library ran the risk of being broken up and lost but, fortunately, it

There were more solemn celebrations when Maria Maddalena Riccardi entered holy orders on 2 October 1720. October 1735 saw the halls ring with joy during the festivities following the election of Bernardino Riccardi as gentleman of the chamber, captain general, and governor of the company of the German guards.

The show went on as sumptuously as ever, even with the arrival of the house of Lorraine, with whom the Riccardi maintained excellent relations such that the marquise Maria Maddalena was selected in 1765 to become a lady in waiting to Grand Duke Pietro Leopoldo. The festivities organized for the 21 May 1784 were a landmark. The Archduke Ferdinand

was bought in a single lot by the Municipality in 1813. In 1815, it was bequeathed to the nation which had also acquired the palazzo, which would remain autonomous for a while.

From this point onwards, the palazzo took on different functions. It was the first head office for the Cassa di Risparmio di Firenze; it played host to the Accademia della Crusca and the Accademia dei Georgofili; with the coming of the kingdom of Italy, it became the Ministry of the Interior and finally, in 1874, it was bought by the Province which designated it as seat of the provincial administration and the prefecture, a function it still fulfills today.

*Detail of the lower left area of the fresco* Angels in Adoration.

# PALAZZO PICCOLOMINI, PIENZA

*Opposite, top, a detail of the characteristic two-mullioned windows of the facade, which alternate with pilaster strips; bottom, the well in travertine stone in front of the palazzo, known as the "Well of Dogs," and made to a design by Bernardo Rossellino in 1462.*

Behind the history of this palazzo lies the refounding of a city. Between 1459 and 1462, Corsignano, a medieval city in the Siena area, became Pienza, the ideal city of the humanists who dreamed of an essentially harmonious city set within the glories of nature itself and in direct relationship with its main elements. The person responsible for this model city, which was based on Leon Battista Alberti's architectural treatise *De re aedificatoria* and Thomas More's *Utopia*, was

Pope Pius II, or Enea Silvio Piccolomini, who transformed the village where he was born in 1405 into a city, his very own, the city of "pious", or Pienza. It was conceived as a large residence where people would live in a sort of heavenly harmony. The palazzo and the city were inspired and designed according to the cultural and philosophical ideals current at that time, drawn by powerful hopes and influential ideas. The birthdate of Pienza is generally accepted as 22 February 1459. It was

*Right, detail of the facade of the Palazzo Piccolomini, constructed in sandstone with a travertine finish, at the corner of the Cathedral on the Piazza Pio II.*

then that Enea Silvio returned to his village as pope. Previously, he had only lived there occasionally in the old Piccolomini family house, a building with neither artistic merit nor historical connotations but where his family had lived since the 12th century, enjoying the fruits of their lands around Corsignano. The history of Pienza and the palazzo are intrinsically linked with the life of Enea Silvio.

As a law student in Siena, he passed a happy, carefree youth in love with a certain Angela of whom he sang in his early verses as Cinthia. From there, he entered the field of diplomacy. Until he was 40, he acted as secretary to various cardinals during the Schism when three popes were vying with each other for the See of Rome. Enea Silvio sided with the reformers who preferred the authority of the Council to that of the pope. He even went as far as to support Felix V, the anti-pope. Parallel to this he led a spice-filled life and wrote. His humanistic writings are imbibed with a pagan spirit which culminated in the free-minded *Historia de duobus amantibus* (Story of Two Lovers).

He finally made peace with the Church of Rome and became a sub-deacon, sorrowfully defending the papal authority. He had shrewdly understood the only way to go in an ambitious career, one that would raise him far beyond the small house in Corsignano. An opportunist, perhaps, he took holy orders and, in a single year, rose from sub-deacon through deacon and priest to become, in April 1447, bishop of Trieste. His meteoric rise did not prevent him from continuing his diplomatic career with the Emperor Frederick III, from whom he obtained the title of Palatine Counts for the Piccolomini in 1448. That year, however, was a decisive one for Enea Silvio because he was elected pope.

Becoming pope did nothing to change his ambition to excel. Thus, he distanced any potential rivals from the court of Rome. Starting with the cardinals, he sent the best or the best-known on never-ending missions beyond the Alps while he openly criticized the mediocre ones with caustic comments. For the same reason, he avoided calling on the many humanists of the time, unlike other papal patrons, to prevent any comparison or competition. However, he did surround himself with his relatives in a cocksure display of nepotism, thus adding luster through his family to himself and his name which would go down in history. And because a noble family is inconceivable without its own city or even its own country, seeing that Rome is the capital of the Church, he set about transforming Corsignano into Pienza and the old Piccolomini family home became a noble palazzo.

The palazzo rises from the piazza, its natural extension, with its sides creating a perspective falsely suggesting greater depth and width. From this illusion of space, the city spreads out as if on a checkerboard, with lines running from the Cathedral, the Presbytery and the Church of St.

*The grand three-story loggia of the palazzo overlooking the hanging garden.*

Francis to the line of the City Hall and the cardinals' palazzi, fading, as if under some spell, into the surrounding countryside, its vanishing point, which can be imagined beyond the buildings.

The works were carried out by the architect Bernardo Gambarelli, known as Il Rossellino; however, Pius II certainly provided the main instructions and ideas for a home that would be fit and proper for a pope, a home that would meet the expectations of a person convinced he was the embodiment of *virtus*, the ideal man, perfection, in his narcissistic view of himself. The palazzo was a mirror that would reflect him, as of course it would reflect his gestures and what he said, but more than anything it would be his image that would live on in the building. Not that he had no interest in impressing his contemporaries with his grandness, but rather, he was more concerned with informing the future of such.

This, then, was the illustrious palazzo, as Pius called it. Externally, it brings to mind the architectural ideals that Alberti had expressed in the Rucellai residence in Florence: a classical style with order set upon order, amphitheater-style; a simple block, unencumbered on all four sides; a harmoniously compact shape, almost a cube, with a partitioned facade echoing the gridiron design of the square in front of it, with which it forms a single, unified perspective. This spatial unity extends into the central porticoed courtyard which opens towards Mount Amiata. This is where the palazzo truly comes into its own with its three-storied loggia overlooking the garden and the valley, a true theater opening on to nature's landscape.

The hanging garden evokes traditional images of the Garden of Eden, with its square plan divided into four, its symmetry marked by pathways recalling the four great rivers of the world, symbolic of the world's belly from whence humanity comes, a reflection of the body but also

The six rooms on the reception upper floor offered the pope one opportunity after another for self-glorification, starting with the Music Room, with its original, painted wooden coffered ceiling forming a crown around the Piccolomini coat of arms. Four decorative beams form four Ps: Pope, Pius, Piccolomini, and Pienza: the myth of immortality linked to one letter in a sort of charade creates an extravaganza that goes beyond being a mere game, projecting down on us, as it does, the persona of Enea Silvio. Then, there is the pope's room with its unusual, turning bookstand for four books, which the fresco of Pius II seems to enhance. And so it continues, with the other rooms, decorated with rare artistic works collected by generations of Piccolomini to whom the pope left his palazzo upon his death in 1464.

For five centuries, the Piccolomini family kept the pontifical image of the splendid home intact,

*The view from the loggia of the palazzo, especially designed "like a theatre, from which the pope, his guests and church dignitaries could in any weather enjoy the spectacle that nature always affords on the great stage of the Valle dell'Orcia."*

of the soul which is purified and rendered sublime in the light that stretches to the horizon. We can well imagine how it was here that Pius found first the reason, and later the love, for the palazzo that he visited six times between 1459 and 1462, when the city was inaugurated. This was the mirror which would reflect his image for posterity, an atmosphere that still enchants any visitor who wanders down those pathways or looks out from the first-floor loggia into the vast beyond.

living there until 1962, when Count Silvio died leaving no heirs. The complex was donated to Pie Disposizioni in Siena, who still own it and who have turned it into a museum. For the people, however, it still remains "the pope's home."

# PALAZZO ANTINORI, FLORENCE

*Right, the austere facade of the Palazzo Antinori, the building of which is attributed to Giuliano da Maiano, on the Via Tornabuoni; below, the elegant courtyard, with porticoes on three sides.*

"Un vin sì forte e sì possente / che per ischerzo baldanzosamente / sbarbica i denti e le mascelle sganghera" (A wine so strong that in wanton jest it loosens the teeth and breaks the jaws). That is how Francesco Redi defines Chianti in *Bacco in Toscana*, and in his verse review of the most important wine cellars and vineyards at that time (1648) he describes Antinoro as "un mosto sì puro, / che neí vetri zampilla / salta, spumeggia e brilla!" (a

liquor so pure that it spurts, jumps, foams and shines in the glasses!) Redi confirmed that Antinori was a byword for good wine in a letter of 4 January 1656, in which we read the ironic guarantee that "those bottles of wine that Signor Vincenzo Antinori gave your excellency in my name were so good that even his priest liked it, which is saying a good deal because priests have fine and greedy palates and Grand Duke Ferdinando used to say

that priests who did not know anything about wine were dull fellows."

Antinori has been a celebrated wine since 19 May 1385, when a certain Giovanni di Piero Antinoro was enrolled in the Arte dei Vinattieri (Vintners' Guild) as an apprentice, and he was probably a wholesale merchant. The family had come to Florence from the Mugello district and Filippo di Antinoro gained citizenship for himself and his family in 1263 because he had a house in Oltrarno. He was then enrolled in the Silkmakers'

Guild because he traded in silk and wool, with a shop in Por Santa Maria. These activities were secondary to his vineyards but all three were vital for the family's commercial success in the 15th century. Members of the family were appointed to civic office and had representatives in the world of politics but never tried to strive for unobtainable

Berteldi. The palazzo had been built by Giuliano da Maiano for the Boni family of merchants, who had risked too much and had already been forced to sell the building in 1475 to Carlo and Ugolino Martelli. The Martelli were also merchants, but were not so interested in the palazzo and had bought it only as an investment because they already owned other

*A drawing room of the palazzo with valuable wall tapestries showing the coat of arms of the Antinori.*

power. Or not until Tommaso, who was elected prior several times and was twice gonfalonier, in 1488 and 1496, and who had houses in the Santo Spirito district.

It was when the family was at the height of its powers, in a flourishing financial situation, that the marquises Antinori took their great step in acquiring a home that would be worthy of their name. They found it in 1506 when they bought the palazzo that since 1461 had stood between the Via delle Belle Donne and Piazza San Michele

houses. In fact, when Ugolino died, Carlo Martelli got rid of it by selling it to Niccolò di Tommaso Antinori.

The palazzo grew when a garden and a new internal facade were added. The facade was designed by the architect Baccio d'Agnolo. It was Niccolò's son, Alessandro, who had it built after buying neighboring houses that he then had demolished in order to create the building complex that is now found on the Via del Trebbio. The building came to reflect the zenith of the political

157

power of the Antinori family. In 1532 Alessandro was elected senator, which enabled him to lobby for himself as a vintner. In a letter of 28 April 1543 that is mentioned by Roberto Ciabani he "begs Duke Cosimo I at the court of Charles V and the prince Andrea Doria to pay 'just compensation', as yet unpaid, for the Antinori ship loaded with malvasia wine that was seized at the port of Messina."

Thirty years later, the palazzo witnessed a melodramatic tragedy. Bernardo, Alessandro's nephew, was Eleonora of Toledo's lover. She was the wife of Pietro de' Medici, the son of Grand Duke Cosimo I. Pietro was not a good husband. He was corrupt and violent but this did not justify his beautiful Spanish bride's adultery. Eleonora's brother-in-law Francesco, the eldest son of Grand Duke Cosimo, arranged to remove the blot on the family's name without publicizing the adultery. He thus authorized his deceived brother to take justice into his own hands and on the night of 10 July 1576 Pietro strangled his wife at the country house of Cafaggiolo. Bernardo Antinori was arrested in his palazzo, on the accusation of having killed Francesco Ginori in a quarrel. These were trumped-up charges that in other circumstances would have been allowed to rest, as the quarrel was a matter between nobles. Bernardo was then killed in prison.

*Two interesting examples of the decoration and furnishing of the rooms, with Renaissance furniture, family paintings, and finely-wrought lamps and carpets.*

The affair was, however, but a minor mishap, for relations between the Antinori and the government remained cordial and this noble family continued to prosper from trade in wine, silk and wool. At the same time, members of the family continued to be prominent in politics and to add luster to the palazzo. Between 1559 and 1760 twelve Antinori were elected senators, including Vincenzo di Lorenzo in 1605, who was also commissioner at Arezzo; Ludovico di Filippo in 1631, who was commissioner at Pistoia and Pisa; Nicola Francesco di Vincenzo in 1700, who was president of the order of S. Stefano, the grand duke's representative at the Universities of Pisa and Florence, and Counselor of State to Cosimo III.

The piazza on to which the palazzo looks naturally changed its name to Piazza degli Antinori, to recall the family's skill at combining political power with financial success in the name of a company that dominated the market and in the end concentrated on wine. And which has survived until the present day. The restoration of the palazzo in the second half of the 20th century brought the building back to its former splendor.

*The garden of the Palazzo Antinori, with its geometrical flowerbeds that date from the 16th century, probably the work of Baccio d'Agnolo.*

*The fountain of Venus, surrounded by ivy and magnolias, in the garden of the palazzo.*

159

# PALAZZO PITTI, FLORENCE

*Opposite corner of the courtyard of the Palazzo Pitti, completed by Bartolomeo Ammannati between 1558 and 1570, closed on three sides, and on the fourth opening into the Boboli Gardens.*

"Wandering through the sweetness of a Sunday afternoon … letting oneself be carried away who knows where by the deep stillness of the shadowy vistas, abandoning oneself to that irresistible heady mixture of nature and art." In 1877, this is how Henry James suggested one should enjoy the Boboli, the gardens spreading out behind the Palazzo Pitti, a noble residence which the American writer confessed gave him a breath-taking sense of history. This romantic vision still affects visitors today as they look at the Pitti, once a grandiose home to dukes, grand dukes, princes, and kings, and since 1919 a museum.

The history of the building which looks over the city from the banks of the Arno started in 1418 when Luca Pitti, a fabulously wealthy banker, bought the home and lands of the Boboli family, determined on building a home equal to the Medici palazzo in the Via Larga. He entrusted the job to Brunelleschi; however, the architect's death meant that the design never got past the blueprint stage. One of his students, Luca Fancelli, took over the project and started work in 1458. The result was the central part of the present-day building, an enlargement of the original two-storied house which now

*Detail of the facade, entirely of rusticated stone, of the Palazzo Pitti, built between 1458 and 1466, and later extended, between 1560 and 1577, by Ammannati.*

boasted seven bays, a central portal, and two flanking doors. From the start, it was a monumental residence. As Niccolò Macchiavelli noted half a century later in his *Istorie Fiorentine*, the home was "Far bigger than any other that any private citizen had built until then." It was a fair illustration of just how powerful Luca Pitti was politically. Gonfalonier and lawmaker, he was in a position to quell an attempted *coup d'état* by Girolamo Macchiavelli in 1458.

The building took on an altogether more imposing appearance when the Signoria, the governing body of Florence, allowed Luca Pitti to knock down some tumbledown houses in front of it. This made space for a private square and the accompanying prestige that this endowed, as it was something that no other Florentine residence enjoyed. Meanwhile, orchards and vineyards were planted behind the palace and walled in, adding a private natural oasis to the aristocratic building.

In 1466, however, Luca Pitti's fortunes met with near disaster. He was implicated in a conspiracy against Piero de' Medici, nicknamed the Gouty, and son of Cosimo the Elder. Luca Pitti avoided being sent into exile but lost his position of privilege among the ruling families. The palazzo, which had been destined to grow apace with Pitti's increasing financial and political prospects, remained in limbo and was still unfinished when he died in 1472. His descendants would make no additions to the building and the combination of the siege of Florence in 1530 and the war against Siena led to the destruction of the gardens behind the palace and the loss of the appealing green oasis. However, it was the disastrous state of the Pitti finances which led to the eventual sale of the Palazzo Pitti and its gardens which Buonaccorso Pitti sold to Eleonora of Toledo, the wife of Duke Cosimo I de' Medici, for 9000 scudi in 1549. The Medici were already in possession of the Palazzo Vecchio, from where the priors had once governed the city and which Vasari had turned into a truly regal home. The duchess, however, was noted for her business spirit and clearly saw that the Boboli house with its gardens could be turned into the most fabulous city palazzo that Florence had ever seen.

In fact, the gardens were what received attention first. They were completely re-landscaped by Niccolò Pericoli, called Tribolo. His design involved woods, pathways, orchards, and an amphitheater. Baccio Bandinelli and Giovanni Fancelli also took part in the work, laying out the central lawn and a new network of waterways for the fountains. After the death of Tribolo, Bartolomeo Ammannati took over and connected the palace and the gardens with a splendid courtyard. It was closed in on three sides and gave on to the internal facade of the palazzo and the two high wings that stretched out towards the Boboli Gardens.

Attention then turned to the palazzo itself, which was expanded, while the rooms were graced by a collection of art treasures. These included a series of

family portraits by Bronzino which Cosimo I had commissioned, but there were also fine works which the republic had confiscated during the Medici absence. Soon the new residence was fit for the elaborate celebrations which, until then, had been held at the Palazzo della Signoria. The wedding of Alfonso d'Este and Lucrezia de' Medici, one of Cosimo's daughters, duly took place in the chapel on 3 July 1558. In turn, on 3 September, Isabella, his other daughter, stood at the altar beside Paolo Giordano Orsini. Isabella had the reputation of being immoral and ended up being strangled by her husband.

Cosimo I, who had been widowed in 1562, carried on secret (and not so secret) libertine affairs at the Palazzo Pitti, which became something of a love nest; so much so that, no sooner had his son Francesco married Joan of Austria in 1565, he went to live there, leaving his son and daughter-in-law at the Palazzo della Signoria. Cosimo lived with Eleonora Albizi at the Palazzo Pitti until 1567, when he married her off to Carlo Panciatichi so he could move on to a newer love, the very beautiful Camilla Martelli, who was half his age and soon set up as the lady of the house. Archduchess Joan called upon her

*Page 162, top, the niche of the courtyard with the statue of Hercules at Rest and, bottom, the* Lion *fountain by Alfonso Parigi, placed underneath a first floor facade window of the palazzo; on page 163, the 17th-century Carciofo fountain (Artichoke Fountain) by Tadda and Susini, situated in the courtyard on the terrace facing the Boboli Gardens.*

*Left, one of the rooms of the Museo degli Argenti (Silverware Museum). Below, detail of the magnificent Cabinet of the Elector Palatine, so called because the statuette in the central niche represents Giovanni Guglielmo, Elector Palatine and husband of Anna Maria Louisa de' Medici; worked in ebony, mother-of-pearl, semi-precious stones and bronze, made between 1707 and 1709.*

*Above, the ceiling of the Sala di Giovanni da San Giovanni in the Museo degli Argenti, with frescoes by Giovanni da San Giovanni commissioned for the marriage in 1635 between the Grand Duke Ferdinando II and Vittoria della Rovere. After the artist's death, these were finished by Ottavio Vannini, Francesco Furini and Cecco Bravo between 1638 and 1642; right, one of the statues in the Museo degli Argenti*

*Opposite, a wall in the Sala di Giovanni da San Giovanni, with a fresco by Ottavio Vannini representing* Michelangelo Showing Lorenzo the Head of a Faun.

brother, Emperor Maximilian II, to stop the scandalous affair; however, the matter was not so straightforward because, before his marriage to her, her husband Francesco had had an affair with Bianca Capello, a Venetian lady who had moved to Florence following some less than edifying adventures. Francesco was in a delicate situation legally for he had been implicated in her husband's death.

Naturally, Cosimo paid no attention to his family's laments. Named grand duke in 1569, he married his beautiful mistress in 1574, but he died the same year. Camilla would only stay at the palazzo for two days after Cosimo's death. She was escorted to the convent of the Murate where she was locked up. From there, she was shunted to the closed order of Santa Monica and had to wait until Francesco de' Medici died before regaining her freedom. She did not return to the Palazzo Pitti, going instead to live at the Medici villa at Lappeggi, where she died in 1590.

Joan reigned at the Palazzo Pitti, but with a heavy heart because her husband's attentions were taken up by Bianca Capello. The archduchess

*Opposite, the fresco in the Sala di Giovanni da San Giovanni celebrating once again* The Deeds of Lorenzo the Magnificent.

would, however, have her day of victory, for at the Palazzo Pitti, on 20 May 1577, she gave birth to Filippo, a male heir to the family. She died the following year and was therefore never to know that her consolation would be brief as Filippo himself died in 1582. It was a sad story that was only partly mitigated by Francesco's wedding to Bianca Capello on 5 June 1578, only two months after the death of Joan of Austria.

Florence; so the Doge duly lifted the sentence hanging over her and sent a delegation of Venetian nobles to the great nuptial festivities which were held at the Palazzo Pitti in September 1578 and at which the new grand duchess was crowned.

The feasting went on for weeks, with banquets, plays, and courtly games in the courtyard while Bianca Capello showed off her personal collection of jewels which, according to a letter sent by the

*Lorenzo the Magnificent as patron, among the artists and writers of his time, in a fresco by Ottavio Vannini.*

The wedding was initially kept secret; however, Francesco soon made it public so as to legitimize his wife in the eyes of the public. Venice saw it was in their interest to be on good terms with a lady who was no longer simply the concubine of the grand duke but his officially recognized and honored wife. Bianca herself wrote to the Doge pointing out that her new role as grand duchess could be useful in relations between Venice and

Venetian delegation to the Doge, was the most sumptuous thing seen during the entire festivities:

*As well as very beautiful strings of ten, twelve or more carat pearls, there were other gems on necklaces, jewelry and earrings; but especially, there were three great chokers covered with diamonds and rubies, in particular the one bought from the Portuguese for 140,000 scudi, so that, counting these jewels and the ones on the crown*

*used on the wedding day, people who understood these matters confirmed that the jewels used were worth not much less than two million gold coins.*

An extraordinary sum that reflected glory on the palazzo, even if a ditty going around Florence then did not bathe it in such a favorable light. It went like this: "The Grand Duke of Florence / has married a Venetian lady / a whore."

On the other hand, it was Francesco who went to work on the gardens, adding the Buontalenti

*Above, detail of* The Destruction of Books by Time and Satyrs *in the Sala di Giovanni da San Giovanni.*

Grotto, named after the architect who built it. It was a fantastic construction with encrustations, corals, and statues and consisted of three grottoes that were decorated with paintings and bas-reliefs; it led to the Fountain of Venus by Giambologna.

Weddings were always the occasion of festivities, however, and Ferdinando I's marriage to Maria Christina of Lorraine was no exception. It lasted 40 days during February and March 1589 and offered real enjoyment to the people who were allowed to

*Above, cameo showing* Cosimo I de' Medici and His Family, *made by Giovanni Antonio de' Rossi to a design by Giorgio Vasari, in variegated white and black onyx; the intaglio was carved between about 1557 and 1562 and is now in the Museo degli Argenti; right, another Medici cameo in the Museum.*

*Two cups in mother-of-pearl and silver, end of the 16th century, probably Flemish in origin, in the Museo degli Argenti.*

take part in the palazzo square. In the palazzo itself, two private performances were held. The first represented an assault on a Turkish fortress while the second took place in a pool specially set up in the courtyard in which fake warships fought a mock battle with attacks and boardings of the galleys.

In the amphitheater, the first Italian opera, *La Pellegrina*, was performed. The music written by Giulio Caccini, Emilio de' Cavalieri, and Jacopo Peri started a whole tradition of operatic singing in the palazzo, a tradition that would become the one truly Italian form of entertainment. Buontalenti and Giambologna were called upon to design the scenery, a task they would also carry out for the wedding festivities held in October 1600 when

*Below, vase in lapis lazuli, gold, and gilded copper, made in 1583 by Bernardo Buontalenti and Jacques Bylivelt. The base is a smooth surface worked with acanthus leaves and on top are the arched bodies of two harpies that act as small handles. Left, a mirror in the form of a mask, in turquoise, diamonds, and gilt and enameled silver, and, below it, a jug in mother-of-pearl, gilt silver, rubies, and turquoise, an example of Flemish art of the late 16th century. All items in the Museo degli Argenti.*

*Mosaic ovate in semi-precious stones and gold, showing A View of the Granducal Palace by Gaffurri and Bylivelt.*

Maria de' Medici and Henry IV, the king of France, were married. For the event, *Euridice* was performed. This was a tragedy by Ottavio Rinuccini set to music by Jacopo Peri; it was, in effect, the very first melodrama and became a national event. On his return home, the Duke of Mantua, who had been present at the performance, commissioned Claudio Monteverdi, his favorite musician, to write a pastoral drama. This would be *La Favola di Orfeo*.

The Palazzo Pitti became a focus for music after Marco da Gagliano (1582–1643), a Florentine, founded the Accademia degli Elevati and organized musical auditions and meetings with singers, introducing, among other things, the symphonic overture, such as the one in *Dafne* which was performed in 1608. Until 1625, the musical group, which included Peri and Caccini, was responsible for composing all the music performed at the Pitti

festivities and ceremonies. Unfortunately, the pieces were never printed and thus none has survived.

With all the theatrical performances and festivities, court life grew increasingly splendid and complicated, and eventually the palazzo simply could not cope with so much pomp and so many guests. So Cosimo II had Giulio Parigi extend the building, adding three more windows at the end of each storey so that the central part now looked much as it does today.

At the same time, in 1620, the idea of a an art gallery took hold, and this would house, among other things, the series of self-portraits commissioned by Cosimo I. The rooms on the *piano nobile* with their frescoes by Pietro da Cortona, Ciro Ferri, and Luigi Sabatelli became the Galleria Palatina which would acquire increasing importance with the passing of the various Medici grand dukes.

*Bas-relief in rolled gold by Cesare Targone representing the* Belvedere *fortress in Florence.*

*Anonymous bas-relief in rolled gold showing* Bernardo Buontalenti Presenting Francesco I with the Wood Model of the Facade of Santa Maria del Fiore.

175

*Right the final section of the Staircase of the Galleria Palatina.*

*Below the Sala dell'Illiade of the Galleria Palatina and, opposite, the* Portrait of Prince Valdemar Christian of Denmark *by Justus Sustermans, part of the art collection of the Galleria.*

Sandro Botticelli, Luca Signorelli, Filippo Lippi, and Raphael would be joined by Pieter Paul Rubens, Anton Van Dyck, and Gaspard Dughet in a painting collection of paintings that ranged from the 15th to the 17th century. It would be enriched by a collection of family portraits done by official court painters like the Flemish artist Justus Sustermans who came to the Pitti in 1619 and stayed there until his death in 1681.

The musical tradition of the Palazzo Pitti continued. In 1626, Salvatori's *Giuditta* was performed for Cardinal Francesco Barberini, Pope Urban VIII's nephew, when he visited the palazzo. Cultural activities extended to other fields, however, as the grand duke was inclined to play host to academies which had no fixed premises. Thus, in 1654, the Accademia della Crusca met there to discuss how the Florentine dialect could be secured as the official Italian language. In 1657, the Cimento, an important scientific institution, would come to the Palazzo Pitti for its inaugural meeting.

Meanwhile, the palace grew apace. Around 1650, Ferdinando II commissioned Alfonso Parigi to build the two long, low wings, bringing the palace to its present size. The garden was adorned with statues which were placed singly or in groups, such as the *Contadini*, or country folk, set round the *Vasca dell'Isolotto*, and the *Giochi*, as well as the statues lining the *Viottolone*, a wide avenue of cypress trees leading down from the top of the hill. There were also fountains with water spouts, such as the *Carciofo*, the Artichoke Fountain, designed by Francesco Susini and Francesco del Tadda.

The last of the Medici focused their interest on the collections in the Galleria Palatina. These were Cardinal Leopoldo, Cosimo III, and his daughter the last grand duchess in the line, Anna Maria Louisa (1667–1743), wife of Giovanni Guglielmo, the Elector Palatine; she would leave all the precious Medici collections to Florence in her will. The records concerning the final days of the Medici at the Palazzo Pitti are dark indeed.

The last grand duke, Gian Gastone (1671–1737), fell under the influence of a sinister character, Giuliano Dami, who kept the grand duke under his thumb by using an infinite variety of tricks. Prostitutes, jesters, and pederasts were received openly at the palace and Gian Gastone, who was nearly always drunk, was surrounded by these dissolute companions and their gross buffoonery. There were also very private, obscene shows and orgies.

The palazzo was in a terrible state, about which not even his sister, Anna Maria Louisa, could do anything. Only when Gian Gastone lay dying on 9 July 1737 was she able to go into his rooms when she found herself in what Marcello Vannucci described as "a pigsty, where filth and insects nestled together." The situation was so appalling that even the flight of Dami and his rabble did little to improve it. The house of Lorraine would have to restore it to its former dignity.

Francesco Stefano, the first grand duke of the new line, enjoyed his title but only visited the palazzo once, in 1738, when he inspected the building and delegated its management to the Prince of Craon, whom he appointed vice-regent. Leopoldo, who succeeded him as grand duke in 1765, was fond of Florence and carried out various reforms while he lived at the Palazzo Pitti, which he set about restoring. The new royal chapel came into being under Ignazio Pellegrini and, between 1764 and 1783, two porticoes designed by Giuseppe Ruggeri were built along the square.

The garden received architectural additions in the shape of the *Gabinetto di Fisica* (a gymnasium), the *Stanze degli Agrumi* (an orangery), and the *Kaffeehaus*, the latter having lightning

*The Sala di Marte in the Galleria Palatina, with the frescoes by Pietro da Cortona covering the ceiling.*

conductors and weather vanes that can still be seen today. A huge aviary was brought from Pratolino, and filled with various types of birds and with water fountains in the center.

In the palazzo itself, the Sala Bianca made a splendid debut, with Gaspare Maria Paoletti working on its architectural details between 1776 and 1780, while the brothers Grato and Giocondo Albertolli undertook the stucco decoration. During the whirlwind of artistic renewal, the palazzo once again held festivities, but now without the extravagance of the Medici. Leopoldo I and his wife Maria Louisa lent a welcoming air of bonhomie to their receptions but left out the pomp and displays of power. They left the Palazzo Pitti in 1790 to ascend the imperial throne. Things changed little under Ferdinando III as he was forced into exile between 1792 and 1814 because of Napoleon, who put his sister Elisa, the wife of General Felice Baciocchi, on the throne of the grand duchy.

At the palazzo, the court enjoyed elaborate dancing parties and balls in the Sala Bianca, and the official court artist, Lorenzo Bartolini, immortalized

*Left, Sala di Giove of the Palatina Gallery, Constantin Feudel, oil on canvas in a private collection, signed and dated 1901.*

*Below, The Sala di Apollo of the Galleria Palatina, with an exhibition of a number of masterpieces, including the Pietà by Andrea del Sarto, the Portrait of Charles I of England with Henrietta of France, by Van Dyck, and Cleopatra by Guido Reni.*

*On the previous pages, The Four Philosophers by Peter Paul Rubens, dating from about 1611–12, and the Portrait of a Lady, known as the Veiled Woman, by Raphael in the Sala di Giove, painted between 1512 and 1516.*

the duchess in two statues: *Elisa con il cane (Elisa and her Dog)* in 1812 and *Elisa con la figlia (Elisa and her Daughter)* in 1813. Antonio Canova also visited the court for short periods between 1809 and 1812 when he sculpted two busts of Elisa, basing his works on the *Musa Polimnia*. Elisa Baciocchi went further, however, occupying with with renovation where she could throughout the palazzo, rebuilding the entrance hall and constructing a new monumental staircase beside the 16th-century steps leading to the Galleria Palatina.

The atmosphere at the palazzo became somewhat paternal with Leopoldo II, who became grand duke in 1824 and whom the Florentines familiarly called "sor Padrone." The Palazzo Pitti would at last reach completion under him. The small, neoclassical Palazzo Meridiana, started by Gaspare Maria Paoletti and situated in the Boboli Gardens, southwest of the Palazzo Pitti, was finally finished in 1839 by Pasquale Poccianti. Leopoldo was forced to leave the palazzo on 27 April 1859 as Tuscany rose in revolt only to be annexed by the

*The Bedroom, with its enormous canopy and magnificent prie-dieu.*

kingdom of Italy. The residence passed into the hands of the new rulers, the house of Savoy.

Vittorio Emanuele II passed through Florence on 16 April 1860, but did not visit the Palazzo Pitti on that occasion. He would sleep there on 14 September the following year, during the first national exhibition of industry and crafts. Turin was still the national capital so it was only after 3 February 1865 that he would be forced to go and live in Florence when the honor passed to the Tuscan city. Even then, he was back in Turin after only a few days because, as Ricasoli wrote, "It was impossible to keep him here." "I do not like being in Florence," Vittorio Emanuele told his son Umberto, "The air is bad for me." The truth was that the king did not want to move until his mistress, the beautiful Rosina, or Rosa Vercellana Guerrieri, whom he had created Countess of Mirafiori, came to Florence too. That came about in 1867.

The king had no desire to inhabit the royal apartments on the upper floor where Prince Umberto and Margherita would later stay for a while, he preferred the smaller Palazzo Meridiana as more suited to his nocturnal outings to the Villa la Petraia, where he had housed the beautiful Rosina. He finally married her in November 1869, in San Rossore, while he was ill with pneumonia, and later wedded her in a morganatic union in 1877.

When the capital moved to Rome, the palazzo was only used occasionally by the sovereigns, first by Umberto I and Margherita, followed by Vittorio Emanuele III and Elena. It was more of a stopping off point than a home to the royals, who had their real home in the Palazzo Quirinale in Rome. Thus it was that, in 1919, the king of Italy bequeathed the whole Pitti complex to the country and the palazzo passed to the Ministry of Education which organized it as a museum. A part of the second floor and the small Palazzo Meridiana were reserved for the sovereign's private use when he visited Florence. These areas, too, were turned into museums when Italy was made a republic, while the palace itself became synonymous with fashion, starting in the fifties when fashion shows began to be held in the Sala Bianca. The Centro della Moda Italiana came into being; today the Palazzo Meridana holds the Museo del Costume, displaying fashion from the 18th century through to the 1920s. The Boboli Gardens, a green breathing space in Florence, were recently saved from the dubious fate of becoming a public park and were reintegrated into the Pitti museum complex.

*On the following pages, the terrace behind the Palazzo Pitti, with the Carciofo fountain and part of the Boboli Gardens.*

*Left and below, the Bathroom, with its elegant neo-classical casts and statues by Giuseppe Cacialli.*

*Above, the pond of the Isolotto, little island, in the Boboli Gardens, surrounded by numerous statues, including the Oceano by Giambologna, placed on a block of granite; below, Perseus mirrored in the water.*

*Opposite, top and bottom left, details of the Isolotto with dolphin fountains and goats guarding the gate, the only way to get across the island.*

*Opposite, bottom right, the porphyry bath from the Roman Baths of Caracalla and the Egyptian obelisk, also brought from Rome, placed in the amphitheater towards the end of the 18th century.*

*Statues and fountains in the Boboli Gardens, with subjects from classical mythology, including, opposite, top right, the Fountain of Oceanus; on this page, bottom, the* Neptune Fish Pond, *also called the* Trident Fountain, *with, a rock upon which are sirens, tritons and a bronze statue of Neptune holding his trident, the work of Stoldo Lorenzi.*

*Some statuary in the garden including, below, the* Giochi, *representing peasants at play.*

*Right, classical figure of Aesculapius and, left, the statue of Plenty by Bastiano Salvini, placed in the Boboli Gardens in 1636.*

*Opposite, top, the* Grotto of Buontalenti, *which represents the transformation of material into creatures of the living world. Thus, from stalactites, bottom left, we move to figures that emerge from the stone, right, as monsters, and finally on to marvelous statues such as the* Venus *(opposite, top right); the frescoes of Bernardino Poccetti emphasize the realistic aspect of the grotto.*

# PALAZZO NOBILI TARUGI, MONTEPULCIANO

*Opposite, view of the palazzo that opens on to the Piazza Grande of Montepulciano.*

The origins of this Renaissance palazzo standing on Piazza Grande, the main square of Montepulciano, are linked with a turreted, Gothic building which faced the parish church (where the cathedral now stands) and the Palazzo Pubblico, the political and commercial heart of the city. Those buildings are still there, on the right side of the palazzo, along the Via di Tolosa, a reminder of how the buildings were arranged around the square in the mid-15th century when the city was in the Florentine sphere of influence, but when a merchant and manufacturing class was coming to the fore. It was against this background that Guido di Giovanni Nobili, whose family was originally from Romagna, moved into the medieval building. Guido's descendants would influence a considerable part of Montepulciano's civic life.

It was in the following century that the building took on its solemn appearance with a weighty covering of travertine stone, with decorative details on the great portal, the ground-floor loggia (then open to the public), the balustrade on the reception

*The facade of the Palazzo Nobili Tarugi, in travertine stone, probably carried out by Tommaso Boscoli, a pupil of Antonio da Sangallo.*

upper floor, and the top-floor corner loggia, which was originally open.

In all probability, the palazzo was designed by Tommaso Boscoli, a student of Antonio da Sangallo the Elder, and was built after 1550 when the owner was Vincenzo de' Nobili, husband of Lodovica del Monte, the sister of Pope Julius III. This was a crucial moment in the Nobili fortunes because, through his brother-in-law, Vincenzo was nominated governor of Ancona as well as captain of the papal cavalry, while his son Roberto, who was only ten years old, was made a cardinal. It was this purple-robed boy who would bring fame to the family name and, indirectly, to the palazzo, which was taking on the appearance of a fine noble home. He became the apostolic librarian and is famous for his knowledge and consummate holiness which earned him the nickname "Angel of the Lord". Barely 18, he died in 1559 and a commemorative plaque was placed on the Palazzo Pubblico of Montepulciano, which had already taken on its present-day appearance. It reads: "As a Christian, he shone admirably in all the moral virtues, but the world did not deserve such purity".

The fame of the Nobili family grew along with that of the palazzo where another churchman was born in 1577, a second Roberto. As a Jesuit missionary sent to India, he went native, adopting the customs of the people and getting extraordinary numbers of conversions as a result. His behavior cost him dearly though, for the Inquisition condemned him in 1613; however, Cardinal Bellarmino, an illustrious fellow citizen, came to his defense and, in 1623, Roberto was acquitted and his method approved. It was a victory and, as such, it was no coincidence that, in 1630, it led to battle scenes frescoed by Bartolomeo Barbiani on the walls of the Salone di Rappresentanza, the Ambassadors' Room, in the palazzo of Montepulciano. The splendid works, painted to enhance the Nobili name, would also reflect the military strengths of the Tarugi family which took over the palazzo in 1713 after the former owners had died out.

One of the most ancient families of Montepulciano, the Tarugi had been entrusted with the

*The Meeting Room of the palazzo, frescoed by Bartolomeo Barbiani with war scenes.*

197

*Right and opposite page, top, two rooms on the* piano nobile *of the Palazzo Nobili Tarugi and, bottom, a detail of Barbiani's frescoes.*

city's most important diplomatic missions since the 14th century. Jacopo and Giovanni di Francesco, respectively in 1377 and 1392, had been gonfaloniers of the city. In 1494, Bernardino married the sister of the great humanist and poet Angelo Polizano, who delegated the running of his affairs at Montepulciano to his brother-in-law while he was at the Medici court in Florence. In a letter, he made it clear that he trusted Bernardino more than his godfather. The Tarugi boasted of two cardinals among their ancestors, and in particular Francesco Maria, who had been so close to S. Filippo Neri that he was buried in the church of S. Maria Nova in Rome under the saint's sepulchre.

The Tarugi wore the habit of the knights of the order of S. Stefano, a title that had been given to Bernardino di Bernardo in 1593 and to Livio di Giulio in 1693. The branch of the latter was added to the nobility of Montepulciano on 18 January 1762. From then until the present time, the nobility of the family has been intrinsic to the palazzo as it has followed in the wake of the history of Montepulciano. It is not the less aristocratic for that.

The palazzo is also important because it houses the Centro di Studi umanistichi Secchi Tarugi, founded and run by Giovanangela Tarugi. For decades, the palazzo has hosted conferences, primarily about Angelo Polizano. The family must also be mentioned for its part in acquiring the costumes for performances of *Bruscello Polizano*, which are held in the square in front of the palazzo. These were obtained from La Scala in Milan, through its director, Paolo Grassi, a friend of the family.

# CASA DEL VASARI, AREZZO

*The simple facade of the Casa del Vasari and, right, a bust of Vasari in a tondo at the top of the interior staircase, with two putti in fresco, symbols of the spirit of* Painting *and* Architecture.

*Opposite, the ceiling of the Apollo Room, with* Apollo *in the central tondo, and two of the supporting vaults in which are represented the* Nine Muses.

*The stones and the bricks of my house settle in together when they feel I am coming home; and the bins and grain stores, more empty than full, almost out of their minds, pluck up courage when they know that he who keeps them as full as they could wish is returning.* It was with this evocative description that Giorgio Vasari expressed his attach-

ment to his house in Arezzo in a letter to his friend Bernardo Minerbetti, bishop of Arezzo, on 18 November 1553. He had bought it in 1540, having fallen in love with a district where "you breathed the best air in the city." It had a plot of land attached, "for making beautiful gardens," and, once the rooms had been built, he made a jewel of the house, personally overseeing the decoration of the *piano nobile* during those periods between 1542 and 1548 when his working commitments in other cities allowed him to do so.

In 1550 the artist married Nicolosa Bacci, his "little lady", as he charmingly called her, and they went to live in the house; or, rather, she did, because in March of that year Giorgio moved to Rome. The pope, Julius III, Giovanni Maria Ciocchi di Monte, was a friend of his, and this meant that Vasari was extremely busy in the papal city, far from the house where, in practice, his "beloved wife" lived alone. This continued until 1554, when Vasari left Rome to settle finally in Florence, where he lived with his wife, who left the house in Arezzo; it became a

second home where Giorgio gathered works of art and to which he retired for brief periods of rest.

After the Vasari family died out in 1687 the house that was destined to become a museum in 1911 passed into the hands of the Fraternita dei Laici, which eventually sold it to private owners. Located on the present Via XX Settembre, it was inevitably altered, both by private owners who rebuilt and redecorated it and sold the paintings, sculptures, and drawings, and by the State, which at first was going to recreate a 16th-century dwelling, and then turned it into the Vasari Archive, with a collection of paintings attached.

Nevertheless, from the eight rooms, and with the help of Vasari's comments, it is possible to relate the rise and decoration of the house to certain moments in the artist's life. There is no doubt, even at this distance in time, that he, with his wife, was the guiding spirit in these rooms. For example, in the

*Below, the muses* Erato, Polyhymnia *and* Terpsychore *in a supporting vault of the Apollo Room, and, right, the painting attributed to Alessandro Allori representing* Prudence, *on loan to the Casa del Vasari from the Museum of Arezzo.*

Sala del Camino there is a satirical allegory of his wife, who, wrote the artist, was in 1548, before he married her, "full of tricks." It represents her "with a rake in her hand, to show that she had raked up and carried away everything she could from her father's house; and, as she enters her husband's house, in her outstretched hand she holds a lighted torch, to show that wherever she goes she carries with her the fire that consumes and destroys everything."

Irony is piled on irony. In the central octagon of the wooden ceiling there is a painting showing "Virtue, with Envy under her feet, holding Fortune by the hair, beating them both," but with a built-in sardonic joke that Vasari much enjoyed: "if you move round the room and stand in the middle, Fortune is overcoming Envy and Virtue, and, from another view point, Virtue is overcoming Envy and Fortune, just as happens many a time in life."

The same applies to the two bedrooms: in the Sala di Abramo (Abraham Room), Giorgio and Nicolosa's love-nest, there is a representation of marital fertility, but it is shown as an artist's dream, because Nicolosa bore him no children and was as barren as Abraham's wife, Sara; in the Sala di Apollo (Apollo Room) there is a picture of the god of poetry and the nine muses, to one of whom, Erato, the goddess of conjugal love, Vasari has given the features of his wife.

The Sala della Fama (Room of Fame) is programmed as a celebration of "all the arts that come

*The central octagon of the Room of the Hearth, showing Virtue, with Envy under her feet and holding Fortune by the hair, beating them both.*

*Fresco on a wall in the Room of the Hearth representing Charity between two open views of Rome, left, the* Campo Vaccino, *and right,* The Temple of Venus and Rome.

203

*View of the Room of the Hearth decorated by Vasari personally, with a plaster statue of* Venus *above the hearth. On the walls, frescoes of allegorical figures, landscapes, and scenes from the lives of the classical painters.*

under drawing and arise from it. In the middle is Fame, sitting astride the world and blowing a golden trumpet, and casting at slander one of fire; around her, in order, are all the arts holding the tools of their trade, and because I have not had time to finish it, I have left eight oval panels in which to put life-like portraits of the foremost of our artists." These were added later and included Spinello, Luca Signorelli, Andrea del Sarto, Michelangelo, Bartolomeo della Scala, Lazzaro Vasari, and, of course, Giorgio Vasari.

This celebration of the arts was accompanied by a love of nature that expressed itself in looking after his garden: "My garden, eager and thirsty for me, but knowing I am going away, lowers its leafy branches, already dried up by the sadness of seeing me go to other houses, lamenting that other hands will cut its grass and prune the rich foliage, the adornment and vestment of the fruitful earth."

Now, as then, these rooms speak of the bour-geois life-style of a Renaissance artist. There is the

*Detail from the wall on the entrance side of the Room of the Hearth, with a painted figure of the multi-breasted* Ephesian Diana, *a symbol of the fertility of nature; below, a scene from* The Myths of Jupiter, *and, on the right, a* trompe-l'œil *door with the figure of a woman reading in the recess of a window.*

privacy that any man needs, or, as Maetzke wrote, "someone who, tired out by many pressing demands throughout the year, found peace and rest in devoting his free time to make his a welcoming house, snug and warm, cultivated and relaxedly pleasing, satisfying only his own tastes and the need to spend there, calmly, the most intimate moments of family life."

# PALAZZO DEI CAVALIERI, PISA

These *cavalieri* were considered the knights of the sea. In their fighting ships they covered themselves with glory against the Turkish fleet during the defense of Malta in 1565 and at the Battle of Lepanto in 1571. The Order of S. Stefano was created in 1562 by Cosimo I to defend Christianity from the Turks and "barbarians," who were mastering the waters of the Mediterranean, and to protect the traders of Tuscany who used the route to Leghorn. It was there that their fleet was based, but their military, religious, and administrative seat was held in Pisa, in a number of buildings which are still in existence, that were eventually to form the quarters of the Order.

Made up of nobles who took a vow of charity, marital chastity, and obedience, under the Grand Dukes Ferdinando I and Cosimo II, the Order became the instrument of an aggressive naval policy; the knights acquired an unhappy reputation as plunderers, attacking Venetian ships and traders protected by the Serenissima, and leaving the mark of their running warfare on some of the nerve-centers of the Mediterranean, such as Preveza in 1605, Bona in 1607, and Achiman in 1613. On renewal of the battle against the Ottoman Empire they fought on the side of Venice in the war of Candia between 1645 and 1669, and at Navarrino and Modone between 1684 and 1688; there was

*The Piazza dei Cavalieri, Pisa, with, at its center, the* Gobbo Fountain, *and the statue by Pietro Francavilla in front of the Palazzo of Cosimo I. In the background, the Palazzo dell'Orologio or della Gherardesca.*

then a reduction in the operations of the fleet, which was henceforth used to carry silk and transport VIPs. The fighting role of the Order came to an end, and it was the Grand Duke Pietro Leopoldo's intention, formulated in 1775 for cultural and business purposes, to use the quarters for the training of the Tuscan upper classes in economics, politics, science, and the arts. This intention was thwarted by the temporary suppression of the Order in 1806 and its final closure in 1859.

However, the military quarters of S. Stefano still exist. They were built around the medieval Piazza degli Anziani, which was completely replanned by Giorgio Vasari. He started work in the same year the Order was founded, 1562, but died before he was able to finish the scheme. Work went on until 1606, however, and saw the building of the church of S. Stefano, the Palazzo dell'Orologio, which was the Order's hospital, the Collegio Puteano with the church of S. Rocco, the palazzo of

the Order itself, with the presbytery, and the Palazzo dei Cavalieri, in front of which was erected a statue of Cosimo I, a symbol of Medici dominion over the seas.

That the history of the Palazzo dei Cavalieri is part of the history of these military quarters explains why it went under the name of the Palazzo della Carovana, a word denoting the course of instruction and training that the knights had to undergo. To be admitted to the Order, the candidate had to be at least 17 years old, of noble birth, have an income suitable for the status of knighthood, and be physically fit. Once these conditions were shown to be fulfilled, he had to pay the Order's Exchequer 120 gold scudi as admission fee, 12 scudi for military equipment, and three for having the family coat of arms put up in the palazzo. Only then was the knight appointed during an impressive religious ceremony celebrated by the bishop in the church of S. Stefano in the presence of the Auditor,

*In the foreground, the statue of Cosimo I with his foot resting on a dolphin, a symbol of Medici domination of the seas; in the background, the facade of the palazzo, ornamented with rich graffito decoration representing the signs of the zodiac and allegorical figures.*

*One end of the Palazzo dei Cavalieri and the church of the same name.*

*The Palazzo dei Cavalieri, otherwise known as the Palazzo della Carovana, overlooking the square from which it takes its name and showing its full width.*

an officer of the Gran Croce who carried out the duties of the Grand Master of the Order, the honorary title of the ruler.

The Carovana lasted three years, during which time the knights took courses in geometry, geography, mathematics, drawing, map-making, and history, and practiced the use of daggers, swords, and firearms. During the summer they took part in military ventures at sea on board one of the Order's ships, joining cruises against the infidel Turks under the guidance of the Admiral, and receiving training in fighting on land under the Grand Constable. The Carovana was governed by the Commendatore Maggiore, who was replaced in the 17th century by the Gran Priore; he presided over the community of knights, while the palazzo was managed by the Commissario del Convento.

Because of its very practical purpose, and because it kept to the medieval stone structure of the Palazzo degli Anziani on which Vasari had built it, the palazzo was not highly decorated inside. The knights' coats of arms were placed in the cornices of the Salone delle Armi (Arms Salon) on the third floor, and the Sala della Scherma (Fencing Room) on the fourth floor had coffered ceilings; otherwise it was like a large barracks divided into quarters consisting of two rooms, its only impressive architectural feature being the magnificent internal staircase, opening into three ramps.

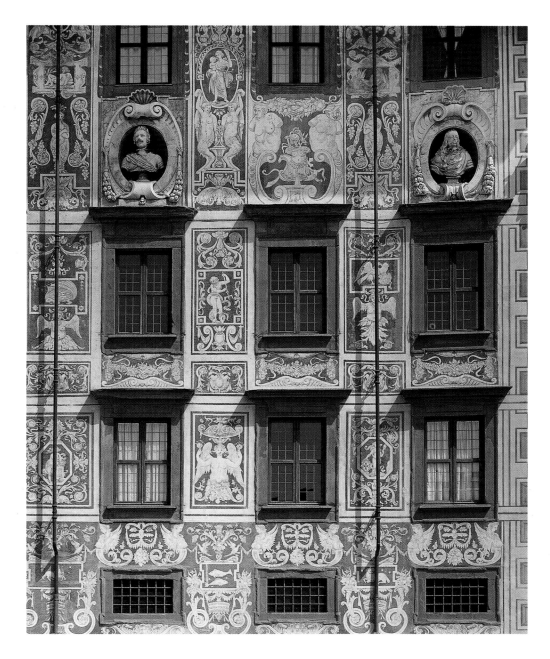

It was on the outside that the palazzo came into its own, with its monumental two-ramp staircase, reminiscent of that by Michelangelo at the Roman Palazzo Senatorio on the Campidoglio, and its fabric of windows with delicate cornices of gray Gonfolina stone, broken up by two-toned decoration representing the bravery and ideals of the warrior, as befitted the Knights. As Ewa Karwacka Codini writes, this decorative scheme was designed "as a kind of 'sermon' depicting both the civil, military, and religious virtues and the actions of Cosimo I in his roles as Grand Duke and Knight of the Order of S. Stefano." The decoration was designed in collaboration with Cosimo I, who especially wanted on the facade between the third and fourth floors to have represented the "six busts of those princes who founded and gave rules to the six orders; these are: the Orders of Malta, Portugal, S. Jacopo of Spain, Alcantara, Calantrave, S. Stefano," and between the windows of the top floor, in six ovals, "figures appropriate to this fine design, which treats of the affairs of the Order, with their epitaphs." The first part of this program was not carried out, and was

*Detail of the facade of the palazzo, on which can be seen two of the six busts, placed in niches, representing the Medici Grand Dukes vested as Grand Masters of the Order of S. Stefano.*

replaced with the portraits of the six grand dukes as Grand Masters of the Order.

There were no changes to the structure of the palazzo until 1777, when the Carovana, at the behest of Pietro Leopoldo, began to be used for different purposes. The internal staircase by Vasari was demolished and the rear facade was altered; but these were not substantial changes. More significant were the rebuilding of the external staircase in the neo-classical style in 1821, and, of course, the enlargement of the back of the building between 1928 and 1930, a reconstruction carried out to fit it for its latest role as the site of the Scuola Normale Superiore.

The Scuola had been founded in 1810 by Napoleon as a university modeled on the French colleges; the emperor abolished the Order and the rooms of the palazzo took on the look of a building used for teaching purposes. However, in 1817, the Grand Duke Ferdinando III evicted this Napoleonic

*The Archive Room of the Palazzo dei Cavalieri, invaluable evidence of the history of the Order from its inauguration in 1562.*

institution and reestablished the Order, even though it no longer had any obvious knightly function. In fact, when it reopened in 1825, the Carovana was superimposed on the Napoleonic school. It became a university course for aristocratic young men, and gave doctorates in law or science and mathematics; though these were more honorary than earned.

This led to modernization of the school, and in 1846 the Grand Duke Leopoldo II dusted off the Napoleonic name and solemnly opened it in 1847.

There was a gradual improvement in the organization and it increasingly became independent of the Order of S. Stefano. On 16 November 1859 the decree suppressing the Order arrived, issued by the provisional government of Tuscany and confirmed by the Italian government. This was the end of the Cavalieri di Toscana and the birth of the Italian University of Tuscany. Among its famous alumni are Giosue Carducci, Giovanni Pascoli, Enrico Fermi, and Carlo Rubbia.

*Detail of shelved archive documents.*

# PALAZZO DUCALE, LUCCA

This was once the Augusta, a fort defending the seigniorial palazzo that Giotto carried out in 1322; Castruccio Castracani, the Captain and ruler of Lucca from 1320 to 1328, had it built. Fortified internally and considered impregnable, it occupied an area within and backing on to the city walls between what are today the Via Vittorio Emanuele II and the Via Vittorio Veneto. The ancient palazzo was naturally the scene of Castruccio's triumphal celebrations, as on 11 November 1325, after the victory of Altopascio over the Florentines, when Antelminelli was proclaimed by the crowds "father of the country"; and, again on 11 November 1327, when the emperor Louis of Bavaria appointed him gonfalonier of the empire, made him Duke of Lucca, Volterra, Pistoia, Luni, and other territories, and invested him with the ducal robe and crown.

After Castruccio's fall the palazzo underwent no changes, and the Elders of the Republic, elected

*The loggia of the Switzers' Courtyard inside the Palazzo Ducale, with a rusticated stone portico, by Bartolomeo Ammannati.*

in 1332, moved in, even though the fortress was occupied by the Pisans, the conquerors of the city. The palazzo became a symbol of liberty in 1369, when Charles IV of Bohemia gave Lucca its autonomy and the fortress was demolished by a furious populace in whose minds it stood for foreign domination. The Elders, the only rulers of the city from 1370, opened the doors of the Palazzo Ducale, also known as the Palazzo Pubblico, and the people, to swear an oath, entered the courtyards of this building that until then had been inaccessible. But this only lasted 30 years; between 1401 and 1404 rebuilding works were carried out by Engherado di Franconia, and the Augusta rose again as the Citadel, to guard over the palazzo for a new ruler of the city. Paolo Guinigi, ruler of Lucca from 1400 to 1430, restored the palazzo by developing three blocks, "the old, the comparatively recent, and the new," the first personal living quarters for himself and his wife, the second an area for work and audiences, and the third "rooms for the family."

It was in this palazzo that Paolo Guinigi fell from power; he had been abandoned by Francesco Sforza, a soldier of fortune in his service, and on the night of 15 August 1430 the notables of Lucca broke down the doors, shouting, "You're a tyrant and we don't want you any longer as our ruler." He knew the end had come, but begged them not to kill him: "Come what may come, but as I spared your blood when I governed you, so you should now spare mine." He was arrested and imprisoned in the castle of Pavia, where he died two years later.

With the fall of Paolo Guinigi the building was repossessed by the Municipality, and its structure remained unchanged during a period of struggle for the freedom of the Municipality that lasted until 1532, when the Elders, as Giuseppe Civitali tells us, "proposed, in the interests of peace and the new freedom, that the said fortress should be razed to the ground, and this was agreed." The south and west wings of the palazzo were demolished, but the rest of the building continued to fulfill its public functions. Then, on the night of 28 and 29 August 1576, the tower was struck by lightning, the

powder-magazine it housed blew up, and a large part of the palazzo was reduced to a ruin. It was decided to rebuild it and Vincenzo Civitali was entrusted with the work. However, it seems his plan rather mysteriously went astray, and the only ones used were those of the Lucca architects who were trying to make use of the parts of the building that were still standing.

A different and more functional palazzo was needed, and in September 1577 the building of it was entrusted to Bartolomeo Ammannati. By November there was a plan for a four-cornered building with a central courtyard; this was accepted, and payment was to be 300 scudi for five years, on condition that the architect was on site for at least three months a year. Having started construction, Ammannati went off to work on other tasks, and the carrying out of the project was handed over to the master builder Francesco di Larino, who was helped by Benedetto Saminiati, a native of Lucca.

The main body of the building was then erected, including the Switzers' courtyard, called after the Republic's Swiss guards, with its magnificent overhanging loggia, and the second courtyard as far as the east wing, part of it facing what is today the Piazza Napoleone. On the ground floor the palazzo contained a number of offices, "for Supplies," "for Victualling," and the Treasury, whereas the second floor was reserved for the magistrates of the Republic; there was a room "for receiving the public," a General Council room, rooms for the "Watch" and the Council of Thirty-six, and a chapel.

Yet the palazzo was unfinished; the north and west wings were not built because of a lack of funds. It remained unfinished for a century and a half, until, in 1728, Francesco Prini, a local architect, carried out a plan for a second courtyard that greatly improved the main building. The palazzo continued to operate very much in a minor role, its rooms used for civil and administrative purposes that were a reflection of the conservative politics of Lucca and the Republic's isolation from the mainstream of Italian history. It had a jolt with the arrival of the French on 22 January 1799 and the setting up in the palazzo of a constitutional government, with a chief magistrate and four assistant magistrates.

However, the status of the palazzo was considerably restored on 25 June 1805 when Lucca became a principality, handed to Napoleon's sister, Elisa, and her husband, Pasquale Baciocchi, who changed his name for the purpose to the rather more poetic "Felice." Already Prince and Princess of Piombino, the sovereigns arrived in Lucca on 14 July, were welcomed by notables and gun salutes, and went to a service in the cathedral, where they were sworn in on the Gospel; but it was Elisa who effectively ruled, with guidance from the minister Luigi Matteucci, who lived in the palazzo. She

*Left, detail of the facade of the palazzo that overlooks the Piazza Napoleone.*

*Below, view of the palazzo from the main courtyard, which consists of a high portico with two surmounting orders of pilaster strips; in the center of the courtyard, the statue of Francesco Carrara, a 19th-century lawyer.*

*Opposite, the Gallery of Statues, decorated with casts and marble statues in the classical style by Carrara artists.*

*The staircase of the palazzo, designed by Lorenzo Nottolini, leading to the Audience Room, the stucco ceiling of which is shown in the detail right.*

wanted to make it into a royal palace, and she rid it as far as possible of its municipal atmosphere by having four drawing-rooms designed by the architects Bienaimé and Lazzerini, with the small rooms decorated and refurbished by the Accademia di Scultura of Carrara. But the largest undertaking was certainly the transformation of the facade of the palazzo's east side; the tower in front of it was demolished and a large piazza was created, dedicated by Elisa to her brother, Napoleon, as it still is today. But the Baciocchi lived in Lucca only until 1809, when the emperor handed it over to the Grand Duchy of Tuscany and they moved to Florence. However, the writer Torello Del Carlo,

from Lucca, was to write in 1887, "she has never forgotten us, and has returned many times to see us," living of course in the palazzo, "to enjoy a few days there, because she felt herself at home."

The palazzo was significantly improved when, at the Restoration, Maria Louise of Bourbon arrived in Lucca on 7 December 1817 with a court that was to energize the life of the city. The artist in charge was the architect Lorenzo Nottolini, and he carried out a number of spectacular works, such as the passageway for coaches between the two courtyards, ornamented with Doric columns and a coffered barrel vault, and the magnificent staircase with a vault decorated in the Rococo style. At the top of the staircase there was a corridor that became a gallery for sculptures made by Carrara artists; and here also there was decoration, depicting the *Storie di Ercole*, (The Story of Hercules), and the *Miro de Pallade* (The legend of Pallas). It shows the Muses the portrait of Maria Louise held by the figure of Plenty. The *piano nobile* has an "assembly area" in the Sala dei Ciamberlani (Chamberlain's Room) that is designed to extol the queen and has her name in capital letters at its center and the Bourbon lily everywhere, while the Sala del Trono (Throne Room) is decorated with allegorical female figures and panels showing Charles V – all to glorify the House of Hapsburg. This was reflected not only in the entertainments given in this room, but in the forbearing and magnanimous spirit in which the queen approached her subjects in order to gain their support, and which was celebrated by the court poet Teresa Bandettini: "Heaven / has no better gift to boast of / than when it raised Mercy to the throne."

Improvements were made to the royal apartments: eight rooms for Maria Louise and eleven for

*Valuable furnishings and statues in the Music Room of the King's Apartment, and, on this page, trompe-l'œil paintings of landscapes seen through windows; bottom, the entrance far right to one of the rooms of the palazzo.*

her son, Charles Louis, who succeeded his mother in 1824, and remained until he moved to Parma in 1847 on the death of Maria Luigia of Hapsburg. The apartments were royal, not ducal, because the Bourbons, holding the temporary dukedom of Lucca while they were waiting to repossess the family dukedom in Parma, were still Kings of Etruria; the former Palazzo Pubblico thus became a ducal, or rather, a royal palazzo. The transformation was miraculous, as Tommaso Trenta noted in a guide-book of 1820: "It is hardly credible that a palazzo used for the administrative purposes of the Republic should have become in so short a time one of the most elegant and impressive royal palaces in Italy. All praise to the August Sovereign who has brought a new luster to the City, and to the remarkable young architect Sig. Lorenzo Nottolini and the others who have, with him, managed to carry out the royal commands so successfully."

Unfortunately the monumental furnishings of the palazzo were appropriated by the Grand Duchy of Tuscany in 1847, and, with the unification of Italy, were dispersed among the royal residences of the House of Savoy, first in Florence and then in Rome. The noble palazzo went into decay and was finally abandoned; it became an architectural shell, and in this state it was returned to the Municipality of Lucca in 1866. It reverted to being the Palazzo Pubblico when it came into the ownership of the Province, housing the Prefecture, the Court of

*Frescoes by Luigi Ademollo in the Palfrenier Room, recalling episodes in Roman history, and showing Ancient Roman monuments; right,* The Emperor's Triumph, *and, below,* Plotilla in the Domus Aureus; *opposite, detail of* Events in the Life of Licinius Sura.

Assizes, and the administrative offices of the Province – a return to its original use.

However, it was also used for an artistic purpose, since the National Art Gallery was opened there in 1875. This was reorganized several times and finally moved to the Palazzo Mansi in 1977. A remarkable restoration was undertaken that brought to light all the decoration of the palazzo: the frescoes, the plaster-work, the entrance gate to the Switzers' courtyard, and the fresco *La Libertà lucchese* (the Freedom of Lucca) by Pietro Testa (1612–50), which has become the symbol of the public character of the palazzo.

# PALAZZO INCONTRI VITI, VOLTERRA

*Opposite, top, alabaster vase and a Venus statue on the landing of the large staircase. Opposite, bottom, the red salon with the* Sleeping Venus *by Antonio Puccinelli da Castelfranco Bottom, detail of the main facade of the Palazzo Incontri Viti Volterra.*

The Palazzo Incontri had not been standing for many years when it played host to Cosimo II, the new Grand Duke of Tuscany since 1609. It was a memorable day. The colorful procession with its long black tunics and robes, the nobles' crimson stoles, the uniforms of the fortress commanders, the short, white boots and livid purple of the bishops' capes, wended its way towards the grand duke along the Via di Castello which goes from the city walls up to the center of Volterra. Leading it was Attilio Incontri, the court cup-bearer and Medici minister who welcomed the sovereign to his palazzo on the Via dei Sarti which was lit up with so-called Venetian-style torches. To the people in the procession, the sumptuous entry hall, designed by the Florentine architect, Giovan Battista Caccini, looked like a magnificent continuation of the street, rising up to the *piano nobile* with its reception room. Of course, the grand duke would have leaned over the balcony to be regaled warmly by the crowd gathered in the narrow street below to honor the noble home of its minister.

The facade by Bartolomeo Ammannati was worthy of such honor and the courtyard with its two cloisters, even though unfinished, seemed to be taking part in the celebration. The palazzo would soon have yet another reason to rise in importance, when, in 1622, Ferdinando II founded the priorate of Austria for Attilio Incontri, a title which would pass down the marquis' line. It would be the honorific titles in the Incontri family that would bring glory to the house, as for example in 1640, when Jacopo founded the rank of Knight Commander of Colle (and that of Volterra in 1646) and two life-long Knight Commanderships which were added to the initial knightly title of the family which was instituted in 1637.

After this period, however, in keeping with a tradition that tended to leave things as they were, the palazzo trappings did not receive any special care. The marquises of Incontri preferred, instead, to keep the building as much as possible in its original state, to the point that even they, the very owners, became disenchanted with it, selling part of the ground floor with the incomplete courtyard in 1816.

Subsequently, a theater was built there, following a design by Luigi Campani, an engineer. It was dedicated to Persio Flacco and finished in only three years, the result being: "a theater so graceful and magnificent that it amazed everyone who saw

it; one that could compete almost without any risk of losing against any other in all of the Tuscan provinces." The technical design of the stage caused admiration: "The elegance of the ellipse is equal only to the sonority of the parabola," stated the *Giornale del Commercio* of 21 February 1838. The decoration of the banisters and the paintings by Niccolò Contestabile on the stage curtain and the ceiling were no less splendid.

To guarantee the upkeep of the theater and to make sure that it would not fall into disuse, the Accademia dei Riuniti was set up on 29 September 1819, and the members themselves supplied the funds to run it. It was dedicated to melodrama. Some of the rooms were used as conversation and games lounges, which led to their soon becoming known as the Circolo delle Stanze, or club rooms, for "family society," wrote Carlo Pazzagli, "which had moved from the parlor to public places whose main reason for being lies in dancing parties and entertainment." In addition to members, "the class of nobles, citizens, ecclesiastics, military officers, and employees of the Kingdom were admitted indiscriminately," so the room "managed to maintain a certain air associated with the elite."

*Opposite, The Ballroom, with two monumental alabaster candelabras, ordered for, but never delivered to, the palace of Maximilian of Austria in Mexico City. On the walls are four marble console shelves, surmounted by cases of stuffed birds, Chinese ivory chess sets, a reproduction of a Balinese temple in wood, a Chinese junk in ivory, and portraits of 18th-century Milanese artists. Below, the entrance staircase, with two sculptures from the Viti factory of marble, stone, and alabaster.*

So, to some degree, a section of the Palazzo Incontri returned to its previous, aristocratic level, even though it was now used for something completely different. It is true that the great musical works and the worldly activities of the club afforded the building an artistic interest which, up until then, it had never enjoyed.

The story, however, does not finish here. The palazzo would again take on all the glory of a noble home after 1850, when it was bought by Benedetto Giuseppe Viti, a traveler and alabaster merchant. His restoration work on the complex was so radical that he even removed the Incontri name, renaming it Palazzo Viti. He added his own coat of arms, based on the tree of life, which featured not so much as a hint of any noble titles. These had always been turned down by a family which was so firmly republican and convinced by the ideals of Giuseppe Mazzini that, if they were not actually anti-monarchists, they insisted, nevertheless, on being recognized in their own right as independent owners of an alabaster business.

And yet, the sheer elegance of the rooms on the *piano nobile* reveals an aristocratic view of life. The

interior is, of course, based on glowing alabaster, but the craftsmanship of the mysterious orient is also here, as are the bright colors of South America, bearing witness to the voyages the Viti family made selling their precious products. The whole is harmoniously balanced by European paintings from the Renaissance and Baroque periods. The walls of the rooms were decorated with false draperies made using prints with holes pierced in them. These sit well with the softly colored frescoed ceilings set off by the hardened alabaster tiled floors that create a truly original atmosphere. All of these, the dining-room, the red drawing room, the terrace lounge, the yellow bedroom, and the ballroom reflect a bit of the adventurous spirit of the Viti as they traveled around the world, at least until 1874, when their Volterra factory closed. And so do the monumental candelabra made for Maximilian of Hapsburg, the emperor of Mexico, which remained unsold as a result of the sovereign being shot in Queretaro in 1867, the stuffed birds of paradise from New Guinea, the Chinese ivory chessmen, the Balinese temple in balsa wood, the Chinese junk made of ivory, the Indian ceremonial clothes worked with gold and worn by Giuseppe Viti. There have also the South American paintings; of the Temple of the Sun in Cuzco in Peru, the main square of Quito in Ecuador, of Giuseppe Viti as he crossed the Andes with his crates of alabaster. Even more, there is the portrait of Giuseppe Viti being created emir of Nepal by an Indian rajah, a portrait of General Andrea de Santa Cruz, the president of Columbia and Ecuador, and fabric panels from Japan illustrating tea and silk processing.

Then, there is the bedroom where king Vittorio Emanuele II slept on 2 October 1861, with its canopy bed, the curtains, and wall-paper from that time. The room brings to mind a similar grand moment in that noble house: the hospitality received by Cosimo II two and a half centuries earlier. The event was commemorated by a plaque placed at the palazzo entrance and shows just how open the republican Viti were in welcoming the king of Italy into their home, the nation personified in the august guest. It was done in the name of the city of Volterra which had voted for union with the constitutional monarchy in the plebiscite.

In these rooms, there is an almost indelible 19th-century feeling given to the palazzo by the Viti family. The descendants of those enterprising businessmen, who still own the complex, are so enamored of tradition that they continue to care for their precious home and have designated the *piano nobile* as a private museum.

So, the palazzo continues to charm, although its theater has been reduced to a cinema, thus wounding its artistic image. Ironically, the cinema has contributed to the lasting splendor of the palazzo: it appears in the film *Vaghe stelle dell'Orsa*, which Luchino Visconti shot in some of the rooms. The film was awarded a Golden Lion in Venice in 1965, which is, in some way, a prize for the palazzo itself.

*The Bedroom of Vittorio Emanuele II, with the canopied bed in which the king slept in 1861; in the center, a magnificent alabaster table, and, on the left wall of the room, a* Madonna and Child *by Lucia Anguissola.*

# CASA BUONARROTI, FLORENCE

"I have a fine room here, where I can work on 20 figures at a time: I cannot put a roof on it because there is no wood here in Florence and I am anxious not to cause any harm in case it rains." Thus wrote Michelangelo Buonarroti on 21 December 1518 in a letter to "My dear Lionardo, saddler of Borgerini, at Rome" from his house in the Via Ghibellina, Florence, which was also a workshop for the marble that the artist took from Carrara for the facade of the basilica of S. Lorenzo.

It consisted of two of the four houses that the artist had bought on 3 March 1508 for 1050 large florins and he added a small building in April 1514. He rented out three of them and went to live in the two larger ones in 1516. He lived over the workshop, and the work was constantly changing because Pope Leo X, after losing his brother Giuliano and his nephew Lorenzo within a period of three years, shelved the project of the facade and

*The courtyard of the Casa Buonarroti, and, top right, the coat of arms of the family, which is descended from the great Michelangelo.*

commissioned Michelangelo with building the new sacristy in the same basilica in order to provide the two young Medicis with a worthy final resting place. When Leo X died in 1522 and Adrian VI was elected pope, Michelangelo had the idea of working on the mausoleum of Julius II in S. Pietro in Vincoli in Rome. But then another Medici, Clement VII, became pope and confirmed the commission for the sacristy of S. Lorenzo with the Medici tombs and also the fabric of the Biblioteca Laurenziana.

It was thus in this workshop-cum-home in the Via Ghibellina that the wooden model for the facade of S. Lorenzo was created, the models were made for the statues of *Crepuscolo* (Twilight) and *Aurora* (Dawn) for the tomb of Lorenzo, and drawings were made of the windows, ceiling, and benches for the library. For Michelangelo, going to Carrara to cut

Michelangelo Showing Pope Paul IV
the Model for the Basilica of
St. Peter, *by Domenico Cresti, known
as il Passignano, in the gallery of the
Casa Buonarroti.*

*Opposite, on the ceiling and the inside of the dome, frescoes by Cinganelli, with the* The Archangel Michael and Angel Musicians, *that gives the room its name.*

marble made a welcome escape from the combined workshop and home and it was even better when a friend came to drag him out to enjoy himself a little, as he wrote in May 1525 to Sebastiano del Piombo: "Yesterday evening our friend Captain Cuio and other gentlemen wanted me to go out to dinner with them, which gave me great pleasure as it distracted me a little from my melancholia, nay madness."

carry out his project. His nephew Leonardo (1519–99), the sole male heir of the Buonarroti family, at his uncle's behest, limited himself to a renovation.

The project was carried out by one of Leonardo's sons, Michelangelo Buonarroti il Giovane (1568–1647), a man of letters and author of bucolic plays such as *Tancia* and *La Fiera*.

*Above, the Room of the Angels, used as a chapel, decorated by Jacopo Vignali and Michelangelo Cinganelli in 1623, showing the saints and the beatified of the city and the Florence area; the altar, on the left, has valuable intarsia work made to a design by Pietro da Cortona.*

He was in fact tired of living over the shop and the great maestro would henceforth occupy much more spacious premises. He abandoned it before the year 1525 was out and all five houses of the Via Ghibellina were rented.

However, this appears to have been the basis of the "fine house in the city" of Florence that Michelangelo intended to build, but as he moved permanently to Rome in 1534 he was unable to

Between 1612 and 1643 he created, in the area of the houses of his great-uncle, a large palazzo with four monumental halls on the *piano nobile* whose furnishings aimed to celebrate the Buonarroti family. As Giovanna Pina reminds us, *we are indebted to him for the acquisition of family portraits and antique sculptures; it was he who gave the* Battaglia dei centauri *(Battle of the Centaurs) its pre-eminent place in the center of one*

*Detail of a wall in the Room of the Angels, and right, a bust of* Michelangelo the Younger, *a marble sculpture by Giuliano Finelli.*

*A wall in the Casa Buonarroti with frescoes by Cecco Bravo, Matteo Rosselli, and Domenico Pugliani, showing famous Tuscan personages, including historians, poets, men of letters, philosophers, etc.*

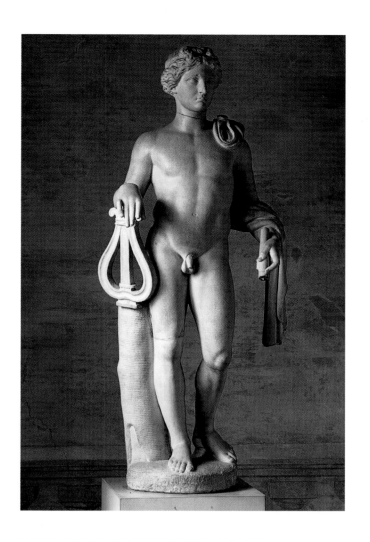

*Portrait of* Michelangelo Wearing a Turban, *aged 47, by Giuliano Bugiardini, and, left, Apollo, a 1st-century* AD *marble brought from Rome in 1620 by Michelangelo the Younger.*

*Another wall in the studio of the Casa Buonarroti with a further detail of the fresco showing famous Tuscan personages through the ages.*

Casa Buonarroti fell on hard times in 1799 when the Austrians, who ruled Florence, confiscated the Buonarroti estate and assigned it to the Hospital of S. Maria Nuova. For the palazzo it was the start of a slow but steady decline. A report from 1823 in fact states that "in 1820 Casa Buonarroti in Via Ghibellina had become a refuge for the most wretched members of the populace."

It was rescued when the property was restored to a Buonarroti, Cosimo (1790–1858). As he was the Minister of Education of the Grand Duchy of Tuscany, he was able to have it completely restored. Cosimo and his wife Rosina Vendramin (1814–56) were the last Buonarroti to live in Michelangelo's home as proprietors. They had no children and when they died the house became a charity and then, finally, a museum.

Nowadays it is "not just a museum" as Pina Ragionieri has pithily pointed out, "but also a center for study and research, with an important library for scholars that specializes in Michelangelo and the history of art in the 16th and 17th centuries." There have also been several initiatives that do the house

*The Room of Night and Day, the ceiling painted by Jacopo Vignali; on the walls, paintings by Pietro da Cortona, Baccio di Bianco, Domenico Pugliani, and others. Right and opposite page, a characteristic cupboard that houses a collection of bole vases of the period.*

*of the monumental halls; it was he who negotiated with the sexton of S. Croce for the acquisition of the altar step of Giovanni di Francesco with* Storie di San Nicola *(History of St. Nicholas); it is thanks to him that Casa Buonarroti recovered the* Madonna della scala *and several drawings signed by Michelangelo, which Leonardo was forced to donate to the Medici collections in 1566.*

The palazzo became the guardian of the memory of Michelangelo through a series of heirs who, in different ways, looked after the property devotedly until Filippo (1661–1733) started to organize it as a museum by exhibiting many different Etruscan and Roman works in the halls. It was then opened to the public as Casa Buonarroti and a kind of guide and inventory, the *Descrizione buonarrotiana*, was drawn up as early as the end of the 17th century.

*Details of the Room of Night and Day, with frescoes on the doors showing people talking, playing instruments, and dancing in front of attractive landscapes.*

credit, such as the acquisition of the Archivio Buonarroti. This was at the Biblioteca Laurenziana but has now returned to the family home: 169 volumes on historical and artistic events starting with Michelangelo's ancestors and going on to the first half of the 19th century.

# PALAZZO CORSINI, FLORENCE

*The 17th-century Baroque facade of the Palazzo Corsini, probably built to a design by Antonio Ferri, extending along the bank of the Arno.*

*The rooms at Palazzo Corsini suggest indeed, and seem to recall, but a monotony of peace and plenty. One of them imaged such a noble perfection ... a crimson-draped drawing-room of the amplest and yet most charming; walls hung with large dark pictures, a great concave ceiling frescoed and molded with dusky richness, and half-a-dozen south windows looking out on the Arno, whose swift yellow tide sends up the light in a cheerful flicker.*

This is how the American writer, Henry James, expressed his feelings in his book of travel essays, *Italian Hours* (1909) about his visit to the Corsini art gallery on the banks of the Arno. He was particularly enthusiastic about the Sala del Trono, or Throne Room, where the ceiling frescoes, the *Glorificazione di casa Corsini*, painted by Antonio Domenico Gabbiani in 1695, are a paean to the palazzo, a splendid Baroque building and a byword for the pomp and splendor of the Corsini princes who built it between 1650 and 1690.

The origins of the palazzo, however, go back further, to the smaller, 15th-century Casino di Parione. This was located on land in the area where the Ardinghelli had put down roots in the Middle

*The characteristic decoration of the walls and ceilings of the palazzo, with grotesques by Andrea Landini and floral decorations by Andrea Scacciati.*

*The amazing luxuriousness of the suites of rooms of the palazzo, with the* trompe-l'œil *frescoes on the walls (right and bottom) and, opposite, fantastic scenery and mythological figures on the ceilings.*

Ages, and which were then taken over by the Alberteschi. With the Medici in power, Florentine noble families such as the Alberteschi had little hope of a quiet life. The attempts of Bindo Altoviti to restore the Republic in 1552 cost him dearly. All his family property was confiscated to become state goods; in other words, it passed into the hands of the Medici grand dukes.

This was how, in 1610, Giovanni (1567–1621), son of Cosimo I, went to live in the Casino di Parione. He had been born of an affair between the grand duke and Eleonora Albizi. Giovanni, an expert architect who had already proved his worth in his design for the Fortezza di Belvedere, the Belvedere fortress fortress, extended the house and added a garden on the Arno. It was here that the Medici bastard received his friends and surrounded himself with artists. He did not, however, limit himself to cultural socializing. He enjoyed the ladies and the gossip sheets even mentioned orgies. In 1615, he happened to meet Livia Vernazza, a Genoese courtesan registered by the police in the *Libro dell'honestà* which listed high and low-ranking prostitutes who lived in and passed through Florence. It appears that Livia was just passing through, but the 20-year-old beauty so

239

Opposite, the monumental staircase of the palazzo, with statues inspired by classical models.

enchanted the almost 50-year-old Giovanni that she was soon set up as the mistress of the Casino di Parione.

Florentine high society, which had become somewhat bigoted at the court of Cosimo II, was scandalized. Only being half his age, the grand duke was unable to persuade his uncle Giovanni, his father Ferdinando I's half-brother, to desist. His efforts to break up the lovers was a complete failure even when the ill-famed woman was ordered to leave. At a tender age, she had been married to a young assistant working with her father, a mattress-maker, and had gone to prison after leaving her husband. She did not have the slightest intention of giving up the excellent opportunity chance had offered her.

The two decided to leave Florence and went to live in Venice. So, strictly speaking, their tale no longer concerned the Casino di Parione to which they never returned; however, the repercussions would be felt in Florence. Giovanni managed to get her first marriage annulled by the Curia of Genoa but, after marrying her, died in 1621, leaving her pregnant. Their son would never become a Medici. The Grand Duchess Maria Maddalena, Cosimo II's widow and governess to the very young Ferdinando

Top and right, paintings in the palazzo's splendid art gallery. Set out in rooms that have been graced by the flower of Florentine aristocracy, it is one of the largest private collections in Florence, and contains works dating from the 15th to the 18th century.

*The Sala del Trono or Throne Room, ornamented with niches, columns, and arches, has a long balcony that runs around the whole room, and great wooden chandeliers. On the ceiling, the magnificent fresco* The Glory of the House of Corsini *by Antonio Domenico Gabbiani.*

*Below, the start of the small loggia on the* piano nobile, *with ceiling frescoes and busts on the walls.*

II, managed to get the pope to annul the decision taken by the Genoese Curia so that Livia's first marriage again became valid.

By this time, as far as the Medici were concerned, the Casino di Parione only had bad connotations. They were not even able to get rid of it until 1649, when Maria Maddalena Machiavelli Corsini declared that she would buy it with all its surrounding lands for 14,000 scudi, as a present for her son Bartolomeo. There were already close ties between the two families: the Medici were business partners with her because her husband Filippo, who had died in 1636, had opened a bank in Rome with them. Since 1644, Bartolomeo had borne the title of marquis of Laiatico, bestowed upon him by Ferdinando II, as one of the grand duke's faithful supporters. It was yet another opportunity to strengthen the excellent political and financial relationship between the two families. So the Casino di Parione became the Palazzo Corsini.

The creation of this architectural jewel would involve several phases. Between 1650 and 1671, Alfonso Parigi the Younger and Ferdinando Tacca, the architects, would work on the building, raising the prospect on the Via del Parione. They were in

242

*Opposite, the magnificent grotto on the first floor, with its casts and decorations, a triumph of nature and the human form.*

no hurry because, in the meantime, Bartolomeo and his wife Isabella Strozzi had gone to live in another house which the Corsini had bought from the Acciaiuoli family in the Prato di Ognissanti area in 1621. Bernardo Buontalenti started the works there. He was succeeded by Gherardo Silvani who brought it to completion. In the end, the Corsini would make it their permanent home while the Palazzo di Parione became a reception venue.

It was Filippo, one of Bartolomeo's sons, who brought about this final change. He was a great traveler and man of the world who wrote intriguing reports about his wanderings. He set about completely renovating the residence as his brother Lorenzo was far too taken up with his ecclesiastic career in Rome to look after it. The latter bought himself a regency post at the Chancellery for 30,000 scudi and then spent 89,000 more to become a cleric at the Apostolic Chamber. In the meantime, in 1680, Filippo started what would be the second phase of work on the Palazzo di Parione. He had Pier Francesco Silvani carry out

the plan for all the land along the Arno. This was a building having two side projections and a square courtyard, with statues and krater-style vases crowning the grand facade on the Arno. A larger, left wing was also planned but never built. On the right-hand side of the main entrance, there was an elegant spiral staircase, and, inside, a monumental staircase of honor with two parallel flights meeting at a landing which then opened out into a new flight of stairs with statues inspired by ancient models.

The project was only started by Silvani, as he died in 1685. After ten years, it was completed by Antonio Maria Ferri. The nine rooms on the ground floor were decorated with frescoes, stucco relief work, busts, and statues, while the *piano nobile* would be a triumph of spacious halls. These included the more than 100 square meters of the Loggetta, the 320 of the Sala del Trono, or Throne Room, and the Ballroom with its mythological figures and other trappings, all singing the praises of the house and the joy of life; there was also the alcove with winged putti holding up gay banners

*Wall of the Sala del Trono, with tapestries of the coat of arms of the Corsini, busts in the niches above the doors, and an Antique statue.*

244

and the mythical grotto with its Baroque scene, a veritable triumph of nature and nudity exalting the Corsini name.

All this was due to Filippo Corsini; however, it was his brother Lorenzo, in Rome, who would spread the word about the marvelous house and increase the family's renown through a series of prestigious appointments: in 1696, he became the treasurer of the Apostolic Chamber; in 1706, cardinal and bishop of Frascati. Finally, he became pope in 1730, taking the name Clement XII. From that throne he brought even more splendor to the family by building, between 1732 and 1736, yet another Palazzo Corsini, but this time in Rome, for his nephew Neri, who had become a cardinal. It was similar to the Florence one, having a library and gallery organized between 1740 and 1770. This was constructed at almost the same time as the gallery in the Florentine palazzo which Lorenzo, another nephew of his, had started building in 1765. It marked the third phase of construction which would continue unto the 19th century and would include the acquisition of great masterpieces. With its 15th and 16th-century Florentine paintings, its 17th-century Italian and foreign paintings, and its archaeological pieces, the Galleria Corsini would become one of the most prestigious private collections in Italy.

The palazzo on the Arno thus took on its permanent character as an art gallery and, by extension, became an ideal place for receptions. The Corsini family continued to use the Prato d'Ognissanto palazzo as their residence. Its importance increased as members of the aristocratic family became more involved in politics over the years. For example, Neri Corsini (1771–1845) was the plenipotentiary minister for Ferdinando III of Tuscany and defended the independence of the grand duchy against Austrian incursions. In 1844, he became prime minister. His grandson Neri (1805–59) was councilor to Leopoldo II of Tuscany, who was the governor of Leghorn in 1840 and foreign minister, during which time he encouraged Tuscany in the wars of independence. Tommaso (1835–1919) was a senator of the reign, president of the Tuscan heraldic commission and mayor of Florence from 1880 to 1886. It was he who nobly bequeathed the library and the gallery of the Palazzo Corsini in Rome to the nation which had already acquired the rest of the palazzo.

The splendid Corsini residence, which is still mainly an art gallery, had to deal with settling problems after it was damaged during the Second World War. But it overcame these difficulties as it would the flooding in 1966. Even though some of the damage was irreparable, it has not affected the aristocratic air of the complex.

# PALAZZO GUICCIARDINI, FLORENCE

*On this page and opposite, the garden of the Palazzo Guicciardini, Florence, varied and rich in sculptures, which makes for an attractive walk along winding paths, past flowerbeds, shrubs, and flowers, to the Boboli Gardens.*

The Via Guicciardini, where Palazzo Guicciardini stands, was called Via di Piazza at the end of the 12th century, when Mercante di Guicciardino came to live there. "Merchant" by name and by calling, he had come from Poppiano in Val di Pesa to engage in commerce in the city. His business prospered to such an extent that his grandson Tuccio possessed a chateau, although according to the eminent historian and politician Francesco Guicciardini (1483–1540), who was his descendant,

by that time the family were "of limited means and estate, being, as it were, yeomen."

The family was so prolific that they almost created their own quarter in the Via di Piazza. They also became caught up in the power struggles between Guelphs and Ghibellines. A certain Rinuccio Guicciardini in fact fought at Montaperti. But politics became the family's overriding concern, so that, as Francesco again mentions in his *Memorie di famiglia*, "he earned the *priorato* in the

year 1300 … and the first of the family to enjoy this dignity were Simone and Lione, who were *gonfalonieri di giustizia*." The family constantly held high office under the Florentine republic, despite the Ghibelline tendencies of some, being *commissariati* and *podesterie*. The family in fact counted 44 priors and 16 gonfaloniers.

The family's political career would continue unbroken until the end of the 16th century and would ensure the standing of the family in the centuries to come. At first, however, the consequences were unfortunate for the area, as Francesco's great-great-grandfather, Luigi, gonfalonier, would find to his cost. In 1378, during the Ciompi, or wood workers, riots, the populace attacked him, burnt his house and drove him from Florence. Nevertheless, events changed course so rapidly that just three days later the populace called him back from Poppiano and acclaimed him knight. This was fortunate for the house in the Via di Piazza, which was restored.

At the start of the 15th century the family lost its assets. Piero, Luigi's son, "was ruined within the space of a few years," as the family chronicler recounts, and was forced to sell some of his property. He was also about to sell the house of his wife, Agnola Buondelmonti, but when this dynamic woman saw the purchaser arrive with the notary to register the contract that her husband had drawn up unbeknown to her she "drove the notary and buyer from her house," and this was providential for the Guicciardini family: that house became the hub of the future palazzo.

The family's economic and political power however came from Piero's children. As they were close to the Medici, they strove to reach the top. The eldest, Luigi, acted as an ambassador for three generations of Medici, from Cosimo the Elder to Piero to the Gouty and Lorenzo the Magnificent, and for fixed periods was also appointed captain of Pisa in 1446, to the *podestà* of Milan in 1449, captain of Pistoia in 1459, and *vicario* of Certaldo in 1466. The third-born, Jacopo (1422–90) was also an ambassador but in 1477 he became gonfalonier, too, and grand *counselor* to Lorenzo the Magnificent. It was he who restored the family fortunes. He had married Guglielmetta de Nerli, who brought a rich dowry with her, which he combined with his mother's inheritance and thus "set up a shop and started to accumulate capital from it because at that time shops were very profitable." He succeeded in buying back what the father had been forced to sell and, at the end of the 15th century, two big palazzi faced each other in the Via di Piazza that were built on the foundations of the 14th-century château.

The houses were run by Jacopo's only son, Piero (1454–1513), Lorenzo the Magnificent's ambassador at Naples and consul at Pisa and then ambassador at Milan for Piero de' Medici. He was to live through the "many tribulations that rent Italy," as his illustrious son Francesco noted in the last line of his *Memorie di famiglia*.

Below, in the double courtyard of the Palazzo Guicciardini, a cast of Hercules and Cacus, from an original by Antonio del Pollaiolo, surmounting a sarcophagus, once used as a lion-head fountain. Right, an internal passageway in the purest Renaissance style.

Francesco was born in Via di Piazza and it was there that he had his first lessons, as he himself relates in the *Ricordanze*:

*At a tender age and in accordance with the wishes of my father Piero, who took great care over the upbringing of his children, I started to study humanistic subjects and apart from Latin letters I also studied some Greek, which I, however, forgot after a few years; and I learnt arithmetic right well and heard something about logic, but little because I then commenced to study law.*

Francesco lived in the house in Via di Piazza with his wife Maria Salviati, whom he married in 1508. He celebrated the event very modestly, because, as he recalls, "Maria was married at home and came at night on horseback without lanterns and the morning after we breakfasted with only the closest of our kin. It was thus because we could not engage in any feast or demonstration because there was a thunderstorm that dissuaded all right-

thinking and sage men from merrymaking." The same year in that house he begun to write the *Storie fiorentine*. On 13 April 1508 he started to write the *Ricordanze* and in 1510 the *Memorie di famiglia*.

Francesco remained in the Via di Piazza, which had already begun to be called Via Guicciardini, throughout the years in which he took part in the political life of Florence. He lived there between 1514 and 1515 when he was part of the Council of Seventeen and then of the Otto, the Council of Eight. He also lived there for a few months in 1527 when the Medici had been expelled and there was talk of reviving the republic, but his loyalty to the Medici made him unpopular with the Florentines and he had to withdraw to his villa in Finocchieto. He came back to live in the Via di Piazza in 1533 after the Medici had returned and had a vital role in getting Cosimo I elected. He was a magistrate but after being deprived of his power he decided to leave for the country again.

At that time the two large houses in the Via Guicciardini formed a single palazzo and were joined together by a double courtyard. This would then remain the distinguishing feature of the complex. This "Roman" courtyard was in the style of Baccio d'Agnolo and can now be seen in the palazzo built half-way through the 17th century by Gherardo Silvani. It was in that period that the compact and multifaceted residence was built in which the Guicciardini have lived for three centuries in the Oltrarno district, on the other side of the river. It came to dominate the surrounding

houses, like those opposite the Piazza Pitti that belonged to the Benizzi and were knocked down in the 18th century to extend the square and give a wider view of Palazzo Guicciardini.

The garden at the back also gained more space. Although it was not large, it was varied and full of sculptures, and extended from the church of S. Felicita to the Palazzo Pitti, where it bordered on the Boboli Gardens. The interior of the palazzo was enhanced by an impressive staircase and the rooms of the *piano nobile* gained the luster that would accompany the Guicciardini family until the present day. These events can be read and relived in the books in the fine library and in the archives in the palazzo. They are records of civilization that enable the different political and cultural facets of a thousand years of Florentine history to be followed.

The Counts Guicciardini who lived in this palazzo continued to be active in the fields of politics and culture even in more recent times.

Piero (1808–86) was a pedagogue and religious reformer, and Francesco (1851–1915) was mayor of Florence (1889-90), Minister of Agriculture in the Di Rudinì government from 1896 to 1897, and Foreign Minister in the Sonnino governments between 1906 and 1910.

The palazzo has still kept its original character of a noble dwelling, thanks to the loving attention of its owners, who have always carried out any necessary restorations. Work carried out in the 19th and early 20th century included the restoration of the facade overlooking the Piazza Pitti. Repairs also became necessary after damage caused on 4 August 1944 by German mines. By 1950 the palazzo had been completely restored to its former glory.

*The elegant architecture of the portico, with the columns surrounding the arches creating a Renaissance harmony articulated by the classical statues below.*

249

Opposite page, rooms in
the palazzo, austerely but
harmoniously furnished
with many valuable objets
d'art, including statues and
archaeological finds.

The library of the Palazzo
Guicciardini, a single large
room divided by three arches,
the books and paintings of
which provide a picture of the
cultural and historical
tradition of the palazzo,
evoking events spanning five
centuries.

# PALAZZO CYBO MALASPINA, MASSA

*The facade of the Palazzo Cybo Malaspina, Massa, articulated by a relentless series of windows and busts on a red background, shown clearly in the detail, right, of two balconied windows surmounted by busts.*

Even before Alberico I Cybo Malaspina founded the city of Massa on 11 June 1557, the Marchesi Malaspina had a house in the village of Bagnara; this was the foundation of the palazzo that the first prince of Massa began to have built in 1563 by the master builder Rocco Fattore di Suvigo. Its main body stood on the corner of the small house over-

looking what is now the Via Gerolamo Guidoni. It was a palazzo modest on the outside, with harmonious classical lines, into which the old house had been incorporated, and it still could not boast of large rooms inside.

It remained like this until the death of Alberico II in 1623, and even longer, as the marriage of Veronica Cybo, daughter of Carlo I, the new prince of Massa, to the duke Jacopo Salviati was celebrated here in 1628. According to the chronicler Orazio Beggi, the grand ball, attended by 122 ladies, took place in a room around the walls of which was a dais with four steps, and "all the ladies congregated on it without confusion and everything went off quietly and with decorum." Shortly afterwards Carlo I set about enlarging the palazzo, doubling the length of the facade and using the extension for an immense salon 24 meters long and 11 meters in height and width. It was a princely room over the portals of which he placed his own name, CAROLUS I. Like any other aristocratic residence, the new building had its own chapel, rich in precious marbles and bronze, statues and paintings, all by artists from Cararra.

The process of enlargement continued, because the ducal apartments were not large enough to accommodate the prolific Cybo Malaspina family. Alberico II, Carlo's son, doubled the size of the rear of the palazzo and it became a building of three large blocks joined to each other at right-angles. This arrangement was certainly not architecturally harmonious, but the addition of the loggia on three sides, which gave the courtyard a Renaissance charm, the magnificent staircase, and the wonderful loggia facing the sea, all columns and hanging arches, made for a miraculous apotheosis of marble. All these works were carried out between 1664 and 1665 by Alberico II, who memorialised himself by having his name, ALBERICO II MDCLXIIII, carved on the corner portico of the courtyard. His brother, Cardinal Alderano, bishop of Ostia, personally paid for the building work and provided the residence with tapestries, ivories, and paintings that were to become the foundation of a

*View of the courtyard and the two-story loggia of the palazzo, seen from the entrance porch.*

*Detail showing the harmony of the columns and arches of the great loggia.*

*Spectacular view of the courtyard and the two-story loggia of the palazzo, with its strongly curved arches and a series of closely spaced columns.*

255

picture gallery, as well as archaeological finds from excavations in his diocese, Ostia.

The ducal palazzo was celebrated by the poet Niccolò Margaritoni, who, in his *Anfiteatro d'eroi Cybo*, published in 1664, praised it as a "royal palace." He starts with the architecture: "The entrance opens on to a spot where is / A charming courtyard, and when the eye / Looks upward, moving forward, / Two facing stairs are seen; then / From the gallery of white marble it gazes at the sea / between the rarest statuary." And he ends with the chapel: "A temple has been built / With a ceiling to marvel at, / Made of marble shining / More brightly than the rays of the sun / In this microcosm of wonders, / So that, what was never seen at Paros or Delos, / The ceiling reflects the floor and the floor the ceiling."

But the enrichment of the palace was not yet at an end. Teresa Pamphilj, the wife of the new duke,

*The bedroom alcove, the work of Alessandro Bergamini, a Baroque extravaganza, Bernini-like in its angels, drapes, and play of colored marbles.*

Carlo II, wanted it made even more opulent, so in 1701 he ordered Alessandro Bergamini to build up the lower part of the palazzo, "to increase the number of rooms, and to give fine facades to the sides, ornamented with marbles and charming plaster-work, all with a noble symmetry."

Thus it took on the forceful look it still has today, articulated in an imperious rhythm of windows and busts on a red backround that, in its deliberate forcefulness, is expressive of power. The interior was improved by the building of a theater, decorated by Stefano Lemmi, who also painted the frescoes in the Salon, which was ornamented with statues and some of the paintings bequeathed by Cardinal Alderano. In the courtyard a grotto was made, with Neptune on a shell drawn by tritons, surrounded by satyrs and nymphs; the rooms next to the grotto were decorated with frescoes which

*One of the four angels raising the drapes at the entrance to the alcove, a masterpiece of Baroque sculpture by Alessandro Bergamini.*

celebrated the four popes who had come from the Cybo and Pamphilj families, and with scenes symbolising Science and the Arts, since these rooms were to house the Accademia dei Derelitti, later called Accademia dei Rinnovati.

The palazzo was then at the height of its splendor, but the celebrations there were to be its last. When Carlo II and Teresa Pamphilj died, their sons laid hands on the art treasures. Cardinal Camillo, according to the historian Rocca, "having a strong aversion to his brother Alderano, chose the best silver, the most desirable paintings, and a goodly quantity of books … and returned to Rome with a great stock of furniture." In 1720, Duke Alderano "stripped the palazzo of the best furnishings and what was left from the sales and mortgages, and took them to Cararra; at this time many of the most valued paintings were sold at the lowest of prices in Genoa."

Then came the French plundering of 1796. Between 25 June and 6 July, General Lannes, who had taken over the palazzo, sent paintings and ornaments to France; a little later the military agent Permon dispatched more pictures and the whole of

*Opposite, two details of the nymphaeum, an attractive work representing Neptune's Grotto, with the god between two naiads, and, on the walls, the principal deeds of the Cybo family in the midst of stucco caryatids and allegorical figures.*

*Right, the Chapel of the palazzo, with a fine marble bas-relief showing* The Nativity.

*Below, the magnificent Switzer Salon, showing the coffered ceiling and the walls decorated with pilaster strips and friezes.*

the library, including some incunabula, which legally became the property of the Bibliothèque Nationale in Paris. In 1797, happily, the palazzo became the property of the Municipality and the looting came to an end; however, it was turned into a sort of barracks, housing municipal offices and records, and, from time to time, military personnel.

The palazzo entered a new stage of life in 1806, when, on the arrival of Napoleon's sister, Elisa, Princess of Lucca, it became again a princely residence; once the offices and military quarters had been got rid of, she filled the *piano nobile* with fine furnishings, brought in all the paintings belonging to the Carmelite church in Cararra, and had the boxes containing the loot of ten years earlier returned from Paris. Balls were organised and plays were staged again in the theater. However, all this lasted for a short period only, and came to an end with the fall of Napoleon.

The return to Massa of the last Cybo heir, the Archduchess Maria Beatrice d'Este, who was married to a Hapsburg, led to some restoration work; but only to so much as was strictly necessary, such as repairs to the ceiling of the Salon and the arrangement of rooms for the couple's sons, who, nevertheless, only put in rare appearances. The most substantial renovation was the redecoration of the Salon with paneling, pilaster strips, friezes, and a coffered ceiling; however, the work is cold and academic.

Under the two Estensi, Francesco IV and Francesco V, the palazzo was not very well looked after, and became more and more like a monument. It only came to life for a few balls and as the temporary residence of a number of aristocratic ladies: in 1832 Maria Carolina, Duchess of Berry; and twice, in 1851 and 1853, when the daughters of the King of Savoy, Vittorio Emanuele I, Maria Anna, Empress of Austria, and Maria Teresa, Duchess of Parma, held tender reunions in which the populace participated enthusiastically.

After 1870 the palazzo was assigned to the provincial authorities and became the seat of the Prefecture; the theater was pulled down and its auditorium converted into a courtroom. Since the latest restoration it has been available for entertainments and cultural exhibitions, such as the museum exhibition of archaeological finds which, despite the fact that the building has clearly lost its aristocratic character, make it still a noble witness to the history of the dukes of Massa.

# PALAZZO MANSI, LUCCA

*The 17th-century facade of the Palazzo Mansi di San Pellegrino on the Via Galli Tassi, and, below right, detail of the 19th-century main entrance porch of the building.*

An unidentified magistrate of the 10th century, writing letters from Lucca to his family in Germany, used the Latin words "Lucae mansi," that is "I stopped in Lucca," and from this derives the family name of the Mansi. The naming of this palazzo may also have something to do with the German city of Mainz, from where the founder of the family, following the emperor Otto I in 962, arrived in Lucca.

The Mansi were landowners and lived in the countryside around Lucca; but in the 14th century they began to devote themselves to commerce and trade, and set up house in the city. In 1502 one Nicolao bought a house next to the church of S. Pellegrino in the Via Galli Tassi, and this was considered the "old house" of the family, or rather that branch of it commonly known as the "Mansetti," which died out in the 18th century. This house was just opposite what was called the "new house" on the corner of the Via S. Paolino, which became the foundation of the true Palazzo Mansi di S. Pellegrino. It was bought in 1616 by Isabella Mansi, who bequeathed it in 1641 to her three nephews, Cipriano, Agostino, and Raffaello Mansi; but the latter became the sole owner of it when he bought out his two cousins.

*Left, two rooms on the* piano nobile, *at the top of the wide staircase, and, bottom, the neo-classical Room of Mirrors in the Grand Apartment, the most richly decorated of the entire building.*

*On the following pages, the vast Music Room, part of the Grand Apartment, with a wall fresco showing* The Flight of Aeneas from Troy *in a highly effective backdrop by Marco Antonio Chiarini. The large ceiling fresco, dating from 1688, is by Giovan Gioseffo Dal Sole.*

261

On this and the preceding pages, the Alcove Bedroom, with the canopied bed separated from the rest of the room by an arch of carved and gilded wood held up by caryatids, with satin drapes decorated with flowers and birds.

Raffaello Mansi was the true builder of the palazzo. Between 1648 and 1686 he bought the seven houses that were to form its basis; they stood side by side and were joined together, but no work was carried out to unify the interiors. It was his son, the Marchese Ottavio, who turned them into a single building, and who added to them five other buildings bought between 1687 and 1689, thus establishing the boundary of the complex on the Via S. Paolino and the Via Galli Tassi.

Overall rebuilding of the houses then gave shape to both the facade and the interior of the palazzo. Inside, the coat of arms of the Mansi, with its motto "Omnes redierunt, Ego solus mansi," appears next to that of the Arnolfini, whom Ottavio remembered in honor of his wife, Anna Maria Arnolfini. Giovanni Dal Sole, Marco Chiarini, and Giovanni Ciocchi were hired to paint the frescoes, and between 1687 and 1691 Raffaello Mazzanti was in charge of furnishing. All this gave rise to the

Salone della Musica, or Music Room, with its platform for the orchestra and a ceiling representing Greek legends in a charming architectural setting; to the wide, single-flight staircase running along the interior length of the facade, leading, on the *piano nobile*, to the arcade opening on to the garden; to the magnificent Bed Chamber, with its silk hangings covered with flower and bird motifs and a canopied bed separated from the rest of the room by a carved and gilded arch supported by caryatids. And then

there were, in the three fresco-painted drawing rooms of the *piano nobile*, the paintings and tapestries that, over time, were to become a highly prestigious collection.

The rooms of this genuinely "new" palazzo became the scene of parties and festivities, in particular the celebrations for the marriage of Carlo, Ottavio's son, to Eleonora Pepoli, for which were written the *Scherzi amorosi*, published in Bologna "by Dr. Giovanni Turchi."

*One of three rooms with walls entirely covered with Flemish tapestries made in 1665 by the Gerard Poemans factory to designs by Juste d'Egmont.*

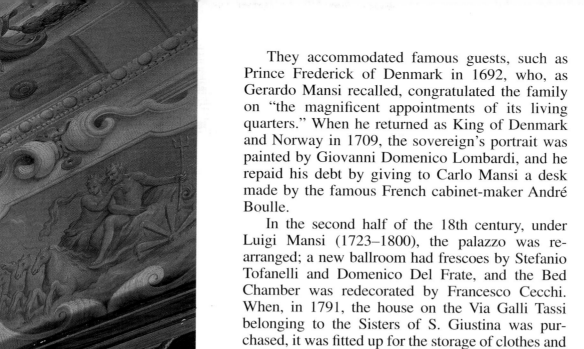

They accommodated famous guests, such as Prince Frederick of Denmark in 1692, who, as Gerardo Mansi recalled, congratulated the family on "the magnificent appointments of its living quarters." When he returned as King of Denmark and Norway in 1709, the sovereign's portrait was painted by Giovanni Domenico Lombardi, and he repaid his debt by giving to Carlo Mansi a desk made by the famous French cabinet-maker André Boulle.

In the second half of the 18th century, under Luigi Mansi (1723–1800), the palazzo was re-arranged; a new ballroom had frescoes by Stefanio Tofanelli and Domenico Del Frate, and the Bed Chamber was redecorated by Francesco Cecchi. When, in 1791, the house on the Via Galli Tassi belonging to the Sisters of S. Giustina was purchased, it was fitted up for the storage of clothes and as servants' quarters, and the bedrooms of the *piano nobile* were refurnished in blue upholstery and the drawing room in light colors. Only then could the palazzo be considered as finally completed.

This princely home matched very well the status of the next owner, Raffaelle (1766–1839), who was Grand Chamberlain to the Princess of Lucca, Elisa Baciocchi; and his marriage to Camilla Parenzi increased considerably the size of the collection of paintings, because she brought with her approximately 70 pictures as a dowry. In 1840 his son, Girolamo, was able to open the second floor officially as a picture gallery, the most important private collection of Flemish and Dutch masters then in existence. Girolamo began work on the great gallery that continued until 1896, when it was completed by his heir, Raffaello Orsetti (1866–1956), who had to take the family name, Mansi. At the same time, the Flemish tapestries, made by Gerard Poemans to designs by Juste d'Egmont, were suitably hung in the three drawing-rooms of the *piano nobile*.

Under Raffaello Mansi the palazzo hosted its last private celebrations, the balls and receptions so typical of the inter-war years. After his death, his son sold it to the state in 1963; in 1977 the building and its paintings were taken over by the National Museum, which was transferred here from the Palazzo Ducale. But this does not include all the paintings of the Mansi collection, which had been dispersed by division of the inheritance.

*Another drawing room with walls covered with Flemish tapestries showing* The Story of the Emperor Aurelius and Queen Zenobia.

# PALAZZO CONTRONI PFANNER, LUCCA

*Right, the facade of the Palazzo Controni Pfanner overlooking the garden behind the palazzo.*

In 1660 the aristocratic Moriconi began to build this palazzo, sheltered by walls, on what is now the Via degli Asili, with the idea of increasing the size of their town residence, which till then had been a house next to the Piazza Sant'Agostino. Living in Lucca since the 12th century as district consuls, the Moriconi were heavily involved in trade, and invested their profits in property that ranged from the Torracchio di Sant'Andrea to the palazzo on the Piazza Scalpellini. By 1667 the external architecture of the palazzo was completed, but it was bleak, without furnishing or decoration, because work on it had come to a halt.

The financial power of the Moriconi had recently come under strain; the family company had certainly accumulated great wealth, and, having created a subsidiary in Poland, it was in a position to grant the king, Casimir, a very large loan; but this proved a fatal mistake. The money was not repaid, and, as compensation, the Moriconi were assigned an estate in Poland and the title that went with it. In one way or another, the company lost money in Lucca over a period of ten years, and in 1678 it went bankrupt. In 1680 Lorenzo Moriconi sold all the properties and fled straightway to Lithuania.

The palazzo was bought by the Controni, a noble family that had lived in Lucca since the 15th century and that was also involved in business, in this case the silk trade, in which it was a player in all the major European markets. Domenico Controni, the owner of the palazzo, had the building extended and finished between 1680 and 1686, and a magnificent external sweeping staircase was built between the first floor and the *piano nobile*.

Here, four large rooms opened out, ready, although the decoration was unfinished, for receptions and entertaining – a central salon, a drawing-room, a dining-room, and a bedroom. Domenico's nephew and heir, Carlo, came to live here with his wife, Caterina Boccella, and with their arrival the house sprang to life with festivities. For example, on 20 May 1692 Prince Frederick of Denmark was a guest, honored by sumptuous feasts and receptions, and sleeping in the Sala dell' Alcova, the Bed Chamber, in a great bed with a canopy of Lucca silk.

*On the following pages, the magnificent external staircase between the first floor and the* piano nobile, *with details (clockwise from top) of the loggia, the entrance hall, and the waiting room.*

In the early years of the 17th century a wide garden was opened up between the back of the palazzo and the walls; it was probably ordered by Carlo's son, Curzio Controni, who entrusted the laying out of it to Filippo Juvarra. It is like a single theatrical set, with a view that wends its way along paths from the large octagonal pool to the central avenue, between statues of the Months and Seasons and symbolic representations of the classical gods, behind which rise box hedges and luxuriant lemon trees, with, in the background, a garden house, no longer in existence, that mirrored the palazzo.

The palazzo and its garden found their poet in the abbot Cristofano Martelli Leonardi, canon of Pietrasanta, who, in a lyric on the walls of Lucca, celebrated it thus: "And then he meets / With charming groves, where the busy / Shear has shaped the tousled heads / Of evergreens that shelter breathing marble figures, each / Lending beauty to the other: / In the midst, under the enamelled green, / Through statues and through balustrades, / Arises, cut in tasteful stone, a gentle dwelling, / Where oftentime the Nymphs and Satyrs, genii of the place, / Take pleasure in the day, / The night, the sinking sun, or the amorous light of the moon, / As it seeks out / Sports and feasts."

Then the rooms of the *piano nobile* were completed; Bartolomeo De Santi and his master, Pietro Paolo Scorzini, painted the frescoes between 1717 and 1719. There is a wonderfully successful *trompe-l'œil* perspective, with gilded friezes and medallions alluding to classical myth, and a representation of the Triumph of Flora, the dispenser of flowers. The furnishings include pelmets of Lucca and fine Chinese silk, paintings of the 17th-century school of Lucca, silverware, and porcelain.

*Opposite, the ceiling of the salon with its* trompe-l'œil *frescoed ceiling.*

*The canopy of the bedroom, standing out against the fine decorated coffered ceiling.*

Here the Controni lived a brilliant existence, made possible by a business so successful that they were able to boast other palazzi, such as that formerly belonging to the Moriconi on the Piazza Sant'Agostino, and another magnificent one in the Via dell'Angelo Custode. In the early years of the 19th century alterations were made to the *piano nobile*, a lobby, a waiting room, and a kitchen being carved out of the drawing-room and the bedroom.

These rebuilding works were necessary because, despite their prosperity, the Controni decided to let part of the palazzo, and the new rooms were designed for a different use of the *piano nobile*. In 1830 it was to house the Scuole di Mutuo Insegnamento, created by the Duke of Lucca, Louis of Bourbon, and later the Court of Assizes sat in the salon.

View of the 18th-century garden, which extends from the palazzo to the town wall of Lucca, a unique panorama, with statues surrounding the octagonal pool, box hedges, and luxuriant lemon trees.

Antique statue of a soldier, and, bottom, two of the allegorical statues of the Months and Seasons that adorn the garden.

In fact, in later years the Controni appear to have had little interest in maintaining the property, and in 1860 the palazzo was bought by Felice Pfanner, an Austrian brewer, born in Bregenz, on Lake Constance, and an inhabitant of Lucca since 1844, when Duke Carlo Lodovico had called him

to be manager of the first ducal factory, which had just been set up within the walls. The factory "was such a success that Felice Pfanner was soon in a position to buy from the Controni both the garden and the palazzo, which, with its vast cellars, was ideally suited for the new brewery." In a recently published article, Andrea Pfanner, a descendant of the Austrian brewer, recalls the company and the early years of the new ownership:

*Felice brought here all the equipment needed to make beer. He hid the machinery and tanks for fermenting the barley in the cellar, and set up in the garden a large arbor with cast iron tables and seats, and a marble counter that was the bar. The Pfanner brewery became a traditional meeting place for locals and visitors who liked to spend a few hours sitting with a mug of beer in a magnificent setting, with an atmosphere that was, as the Lucca writer Gugliemo Petroni has suggested, a reminder of that immortalized in Renoir's* Moulin de la Galette. *The shrewd brewer, Felice Pfanner, went about his business in this* Belle Époque *environment, and now and again he amused himself by artificially freezing the beer tank so that he could skate on it and remind himself of the times when, as a child, he used to skate on Lake Constance.*

The brewery closed in 1929, but the palazzo has remained in the possession of Felice Pfanner's descendants until the present day, used as a home by five generations of the family. Pietro, Felice's son, was mayor of Lucca from 1920 to 1922, and his nephew Alessandro was Director of the

*Two symbolic statues of classical divinities in front of the fountain of this wonderful garden, the work of Filippo Juvarra.*

Psychiatric Hospital of Maggiano. The palazzo has continued to have its moments of glory, such as immediately after the Second World War, when the salon was the setting for a grand ceremony welcoming the return of the Foreign Minister, Carlo Sforza, a relative of the family, from his exile in America. Between 1930 and 1960, on the Feast of the Holy Cross, three members of the Roman Curia slept in the bedroom on the *piano nobile*: Cardinal Camerlengo Lauri, Cardinal Pellegrinetti, and Archbishop Volpi. Between 1980 and 1990, the rooms of the *piano nobile* hosted the Exhibition of Historic Costume of the 18th and 19th centuries, organized by the Municipality of Lucca, and this use for an artistic purpose lent distinction to the palazzo.

Between 1995 and 1999, restoration work was carried out, to ensure that the rooms of the *piano nobile* were properly set up for exhibitions and cultural events. The judgment of André Suarès, the Marseillaise writer, is as true today as it was when he made it in the twenties: "with its theatrical staircase and coffer-ceilinged hall that merges in the distance into an attractive view of the garden greenery outside, it seems built for putting on entertainments." The proof of this is that the palazzo and its garden have been used as a film and television set, and several critically acclaimed films were made there: *Arrivano i bersaglieri* by Luigi Magni in 1980, *Il Marchese del Grillo* by Mario Monicelli in 1981, and the well-known *Portrait of a Lady* by Jane Campion in 1996.

# PALAZZO CHIGI SARACINI, SIENA

*The great pile of the Palazzo Chigi Saracini on the Via di Città, Siena. Right, detail of the courtyard with its triple-mullioned windows and Ghibellini blackbirds.*

The tower that rises up on the bend in the Via di Città was already there when in 1163 the Marescotti, feudatories of Maremma, arrived in Siena from Montepescali and built a house backing on to it. Like true Ghibellines, they ostentatiously placed a row of blackbirds, the Ghibelline emblem, on its walls, and immediately demonstrated their political resolution by making this house the seat of the city magistrates before the Palazzo Pubblico was built.

From this house the Marescotti pursued a policy unreservedly pro-imperial and they managed to obtain from the emperor the privilege of striking coins in the Bulgano, the Sienese mint. It was a policy dedicated, in defense of municipal independence, to military confrontation with the Guelphs. This came to a head in the battle of Montaperti on 14 September 1260, when the Sienese defeated the Florentines. Indirectly, the tower became a player in this event. "As it was high and only a round platform," wrote Cerreto Ciccolini, "he went up to the top of the Marescotti tower, from where it was possible to see all our men and those of the Florentine camp... and most of the people were at the foot of the tower, kneeling and praying God and our Holy Virgin Mary to give our soldiers strength and vigor against our enemies, those cursed Florentine dogs."

So legend began to surround the tower, both in written history and in popular tradition. It was not until 50 years later that the Guelphs and the Ghibelline Marescotti gave up political battle to dedicate themselves to business and ecclesiastical affairs. The palazzo, with its tower, returned to normal life, an existence lacking in outstanding moments. Nevertheless, decoration of it continued.

About 1460 the brothers Rinaldo and Jacopo rebuilt it and enriched the interior with fittings and furniture. The building work was in line with the replanning of Siena, but the palazzo retained its Gothic style. This was the last time the Marescotti were able to undertake such works, because soon afterwards their fortunes waned and they had to sell the palazzo.

*Entrance portal to the Accademia Chigiana, built in a simple Renaissance style, with busts in the oval wall niches.*

*Bambino* (Madonna and Child), attributed to Donatello, and the relief *La discordia* (Discord) by Francesco di Giorgio. This look, artistic, cultured, and refined, was to remain indelibly associated with it for the next two-and-a-half centuries of Piccolomini-Mandoli occupation, until between 1770 and 1786 it was sold, wing by wing, to a new owner, Marco Antonio Saracini.

Under the new owner the facade on the Via di Città was extended upwards by another line of triplemullioned windows and the *piano nobile* was

*Opposite, view of a corner of the Dining Room with its fine coffered ceiling.*

*Left and below, details of the Drawing Room and Small Drawing Room, evidence of a refined taste in furnishings, with its drapes, carpets, and valuable furniture.*

It was bought in 1506 by a branch of the Piccolomini, the Mandoli, who made no changes to the architecture of the exterior, but turned the interior into a royal palace. The first-floor loggia was enriched with an airy decoration of grotesque figures by Giorgio di Giovanni, and in the rooms of the north wing of the palazzo the family that had taken over from the Marescotti was celebrated. The painters Arcangelo Salimbeni and M. Tiberio Billò were hired to glorify the deeds of the Piccolomini in 15 paintings placed in tondi and rectangles, the details of which were agreed in advance with Girolamo Mandoli, as is shown by a "schedule of ornament" dated 2 May 1474. In fact, nothing was left to chance or artistic invention, and the events depicted were precisely those indicated by the buyer, who wanted the paintings to be a seal on his historic appropriation of the palazzo. These family deeds, moreover, were presented in a highly cultural framework; other rooms were crowned with 18 paintings in tondi and ovals recalling Greek and Roman legends, with nine episodes from the fable of Cupid and Psyche, and 58 events from the history of Ancient Rome, a city the Piccolomini liked to identify with through the family popes, Pius II and Pius III.

Thus the interior of the palazzo took on a decidedly new look, revealing the artistic taste of the Piccolomini, and an art collection was started that was notable, in particular, for its *Madonna col*

covered with stone; but it was his brother, Galgano Saracini (1752–1824), who added to the aristocratic ambiance of the rooms, changing them to fit his own taste and establishing the arrival of the new family by expunging evidence of the previous owners. The celebrations of family history in the salons were now of the Saracini, Antonio Caselletti and Francesco Paccagnani having covered the 16th-century frescoes and replaced them with paintings of famous members of the new line.

The chapel was built in 1787 in the right wing of the courtyard; it was designed by Giuseppe Mazzuoli and constructed with materials recovered from the suppressed oratory of the Compagnia di San Giovanni Battista della Morte, in an art salvage operation that was quite unusual for the time. The altar fresco was cut out and, with its two statues of the *Annunciata* and the *Angelo*, was transported to the palazzo. This was a sign of Galgano Saracini's great passion for art collecting, which led him to enlarge the collection begun by Bernardino in 1776 and which reached its zenith with the setting up of what was no less than a full art gallery of 20 rooms on the *piano nobile* of the palazzo. This was furnished with sculptures of members of the family in Roman dress by Barbato Cipriani and Giovanni Rasi, and ancestral busts of Paolo V and Giovanni Michele Saracini commissioned from Pietro Bienaimé.

"Galgano's main concern," wrote Carlo Sisi, "was to bring together works from the churches and palazzi of Siena and from the contemporary market, and arrange them in an organic order in which the masterpiece and the minor work could, as far as possible, stand side by side as equally worthy; this was why he requested his many collaborators to clean paintings, reshape cornices, and repair sculptures almost to the point of forgery." Many archaeological finds from excavations in Siena, Volterra, and Chiusi found their place next to the masterpieces of 16th and 17th-century painting.

Alessandro Saracini (1807–77), Galgano's son, continued in his father's tradition, as we are told by the inscription on his bust that describes him as "mecenas alter" (another Maecenas); he covered the Piccolomini frescoes with tapestries and filled the rooms with magnificent furniture, lamps, and hangings that erased any relationship with the previous family and gave them an air of great elegance. The sole exception to this scheme was the Ballroom, greatly extended now to two floors and newly decorated with frescoes glorifying the

*Opposite and below, fine furniture, chandeliers, consoles, mirrors, and vases make up the rich furnishing of the Conversation Room on the piano nobile.*

Saracini that reached to the ceiling, wherein was depicted the *Rotta data da' Senesi fuori porta Camollia* (The Defeat Inflicted outside the Camollia Gate) on 25 July 1526 on the army of Clement VII, a victory in which Girolamo and Gherardo, ancestors of the Saracini, had distinguished themselves.

Having no direct heirs, Alessandro Saracini bequeathed the palazzo and all its contents to his nephew Fabio, Count Chigi (1849–1906), on condition that he took the family name Saracini; the palazzo was from then on called the Palazzo Chigi Saracini, and it found its new Maecenas in Fabio's nephew, Count Guido (1880–1965), who had a genuine vocation for music, and gave it a rather different artistic image from the one it had before. The Ballroom became a concert hall and was suitably renovated in 1914 by Arturo Viligiardi. The 18th-century frescoes saw the light of day again, the four doors were painted with representations of famous composers, and on the ceiling was depicted *Il ritorno dei Senesi vittoriosi da Montaperti* (The Return of the Victorious Sienese from Montaperti). This linked the past glory of the tower to that of the present palazzo, dedicated as it now was to the art of music, as Fulvio Corsini's statues of *Armonia, Harmony*, and *Melodia, Melody*, testified.

*Two more of the palazzo's magnificent rooms, showing the refinement of furnishings in the Renaissance Drawing Room/Study and the Imperial-style bedroom.*

This hall very soon became the cradle of music in Siena and was to achieve international fame. It began with concerts by the music association "Micat in vertice," which Guido Chigi Saracini founded to give the palazzo a specifically musical purpose. In 1932 the Count founded the Accademia Musicale Chigiana, which immediately fulfilled a role at European level; and subsequently he untiringly promoted a series of initiatives, some including himself as composer. In 1939 he founded the Chigiano Quartet and started the Settimane Musicali Senesi, the Sienese Weeks of Music, both of which still take place today; in 1950 the Madrigalisti group was formed under the direction of Andrea Morosini.

The palazzo was thus fully dedicated to music and was destined to outgrow its owner; it is the seat of the Fondazione Chigiana, incorporated in 1960, and now a kind of music university, a center for musical studies, with courses that include seminars, concerts by famous artists, and conferences. The palazzo is one of Siena's main cultural boasts, and Italy's too.

*Detail of the frescoed and stucco-decorated ceiling of the Concert Hall of the Accademia Musicale Chigiana, by the painter, sculptor, and architect Arturo Viligiardi, who was responsible for the rebuilding and decoration of the whole hall; the large central fresco shows* The Return of the Victorious Sienese from the Battle of Montaperti.

Some of the works in the Chigi Saracini Art Gallery, including many fine examples of Sienese art, such as stucco and marble bas-reliefs, enamels and frescoes mainly of sacred subjects. Clockwise from the left, Beatrice and Dante *by Giovanni Duprè*; Madonna and Child *by the Master of the Piccolomini Madonna*; Saint Jerome, *by Domenico Beccafumi*; Saint Jerome, *by Gian Lorenzo Bernini. Opposite, (1)* Giovanni I, *by an unknown Tuscan sculptor; (2)* The Child Jesus, *by Giovanni Battista Foggini; (3)* Madonna and Child, *by Urbano da Cortona; (4)* The Deposition of Christ, *by Giuseppe Mazzuoli; (5)* Angel, *from the workshop of Gano di Fazio.*

1

3

4

2

5

# PALAZZO BIANCHI-BANDINELLI, SIENA

*The courtyard of the Palazzo Bianchi Bandinelli, with the statue of* Hercules *below, and, right, an interior stair landing.*

This is not the noble house of a family that has for centuries been at the summit of the cultural and political life of Siena; it is exclusively a manifestation of the opulence and power, the worldliness and art that Giulio Bianchi Bandinelli created in his own image and likeness. He was a major figure in Napoleonic Siena, chamberlain to the Queen of

Etruria in 1804, mayor of the city in 1810, and prefect of the district of Ombrone in 1814; during the Restoration he was a governor and lieutenant-general of the Lorraine grand duke of Tuscany.

The building of the palazzo, which took in an isolated area beyond the Ponte di Romana, was designed to mirror the personality, celebrating the characteristic features of neo-classical art, beauty and grace, as the criteria of grandeur. The facade was a wide surface modeled in the Renaissance style "with all its ironwork on the first floor," and the graceful entrance porch opened into a vestibule subdivided by three elliptical arches and leading into a courtyard decorated with busts of antique form, placed around the walls so as to form a crown for the statue of *Ercole*, or Hercules. It is immediately clear that the architectural aim is a "finely ornamented" exterior, which Bianchi wanted reflected in the surrounding area; in 1803 he renovated at his own expense the facades of eight "ugly" black cottages, so that the whole of the Via Roma would blend with his own residence.

The classical image of the exterior is repeated at the back of the palazzo by a facade in the form of a vestibule of an Ionic temple that opens on to a radiant garden ornamented with antique statues and classicizing architectural features. The garden was developed in 1811 when the greenery was modeled on "a wood in the French style," with a series of lines of trees alternating with quincunx, and suggestive of Versailles; paths between the hedges and the orange-trees are marked out with busts and benches, and the Sphinxes, inscrutable guardians of the ancient mysteries suggested by the two Doric temples, recall an esoteric past.

The triumphant interior has a suite of rooms on the *piano nobile* that included a theater, no longer in existence, but which still rejoices in the frescoes of Luigi Ademollo: they breathe the grace and Olympian calm of the Greek and Roman myths, the *Nozze di Alessandro e Rossana* (The Marriage of Alexander and Roxana) and the *Sacrifici di Numa* (The Sacrifices of Numa). In contrast with these is the "forest" room where a decoration of buildings and scenes of nature merges into endless greenery, creating illusory scenic prospects that rise to the changing sky of the ceiling and are lost in the dream-like images of the garden outside.

*The fine Entrance Hall to the* piano nobile, *with stucco decorations by Pietro Rossi.*

293

All this is reflected in furnishing that is in harmony with the neo-classical spirit: the decoration in the Chippendale style of the ceilings of the central Salon and the Oval Room; the griffins and garlands of flowers painted by Pietro Rossi; the furniture in the English style, and the avant-garde inlay work by which Antonio Rosi made his name.

The palazzo was solemnly opened in January 1804, as the writer Antonio Francesco Bandini noted in his *Diario* or Diary, by a "gathering" and "French country dances," which took place in the stalls of the theater, while gaming-tables were set out in the drawing rooms, with "dicing cups, clocks, and furniture in the best taste," alternatives to the "buffet where all sorts of refreshment were served." But, naturally, the guests were free to rove the courtyard and the garden in the light of the lamps, where there was always a serving-girl "dressed in the French style" to help them, or children, "dressed as gardeners, with garlands of flowers on their heads or elsewhere," who gave out lilies of the valley and anemones to the ladies and sweet violets to the gentlemen.

This was the first of the many parties given in the palazzo, all, according to Bandini, reporting the opinion of the Marchese Guadagni, excellent "for their gentility, elegance, and charm." This was an opinion shared by all the nobility of Siena, and indeed not only the Sienese, to judge by the comments of the Queen of Etruria, guest of honor at a party in August 1804, who said that the palazzo

"was like a paradise." The historians also tell of an extraordinary occasion, in September 1804, which Bianchi organized in the chapel, with its frescoes by Liborio Guerrini, as if to celebrate the sacred building as an aristocratic precious object. In fact, the chapel was to become a symbol of Bianchi's artistic patronage, and in 1812, as Carlo Sisi recalls, he made of it "a small sanctuary of artistic relics of the city brought from institutions suppressed under Napoleonic rule also commissioning works from artists who had already worked in the palazzo." Thus *L'Assunzione della Virgine* (The Assumption of the Virgin) by Jacopo Ligozzi came from Monte Oliveto Maggiore, to replace the vault fresco by Guerrini. The statue of *Beato Bernardo* (Blessed Bernard) by Pasquale Bocciardo also came from there, while from the Monastero di Ognissanti, demolished to build the garden, came the painting of the *Vergine*

*This page and opposite, bottom, views of the rooms on the* piano nobile *of the palazzo entirely frescoed by Luigi Ademollo in the early years of the 19th century with mythological subjects, including griffins and garlands of flowers, and some "woodland" decoration from a series of* trompe-l'œil *landscapes.*

*Opposite above, another detail of the Entrance Hall, showing the stucco work.*

*An eagle decoration in the "woodland" room.*

*del Presepe* (Virgin of the Stable), which gave its name to the chapel. Then Vincenzo Dei renovated the decoration and Pietro Rossi made busts of the Sienese popes *Alessandro III*, the pope of the Rolando Bandinelli family, and *Alessandro VII* of the house of Chigi.

Like the chapel, the theater was the scene of Giulio Bianchi's patronage, and well-known plays by Pietro Metastasio, Carlo Goldoni, and Vittorio Alfieri were played there. In August 1818, the Grand Duke Ferdinando III of Tuscany visited Siena, was rapturously welcomed at the palazzo, and attended performances of two plays by Goldoni, *Il cavaliere di spirito* and *L'Apatista*.

But that was not the full extent of the patron's diplomatic skill, because in the garden, where the

together in friendship to pursue their gradual improvement of themselves."

For this reason the palazzo on the Via Roma can be considered the home exclusively of Giulio Bianchi Bandinelli, or, as has also been said, "the home of everyone," given the cultural and social message it promoted. His son, Mario Bianchi, did not take account of this, and preferred to build outside the Porta Romana a modest villa dedicated to practicality and suited to a very private daily life.

*Left, sculpture of a* Sphynx *in the garden behind the palazzo.*

*Neo-classical facade of the palazzo facing on to the garden, in the form of the vestibule of a Greek Ionic temple.*

reception took place, there was a small Tuscan temple dedicated to the grand duke, carrying the words "Alla Risconoscenza" (In Gratitude). When the *Gazzetta di Firenze* reported the grand duke's visit on 5 September, the residence was referred to as "The enchanted palace of Alcina."

*Noblesse oblige* and patronage were expended not only on festivities in the palazzo, but in cultural and social enterprises that benefited Siena. When he died they were duly remembered on 28 August 1824 in the funeral address given by Father Massimiliano Ricca in the Servite church, as Carlo Sisi recalls:

*He was praised as a conservator of monuments, restored 'with care and seriousness' and 'without compromising by discordant alterations' their original structure; as the restorer of the 'national' Palio race, which had been stripped of its medieval heritage and dressed up in ancient Roman guise; he promoted the institutions of the city, including the new Sienese Athenaeum, the building of the Collegio Tolomei, the 'elegant cutting down' of the Accademia dei Fisiocritici, the 'settled home' given to the Accademia Tegea, the establishment of the Art Gallery in the Institute of Fine Arts and the Public Library, and the establishment of the Municipal Orphanage, a fine example of modern philanthropy.*

Giulio Bianchi, with his love of life, as shown in the magnificence of his palazzo, celebrated culture and good taste not as an end in itself, in which the arts were "purely an ornament" for his home, but as a "means for forwarding a great political purpose," according to the words of Francesco Antonio Mori, spoken at the solemn exequy in S. Agostino on 16 September 1824: "since imitation of ideal Beauty makes men more gentle, they come

# PALAZZO BORGHESE, FLORENCE

*Detail of the facade of the Palazzo Borghese on the Via Ghibellina, with an Ionic pediment and winged victories surmounting the 15th-century gray stone front; right, neo-classical stone post in front of the palazzo.*

It all started at a ball that was part of the celebrations organized in March 1821 by the Comune of Florence to welcome the prince Camillo Borghese, the husband of Pauline Bonaparte, from whom he was already separated. He moved to Florence from Rome, going to live in the 15th-century Palazzo Salviati, which he had inherited from his mother, the last of the noble Salviati line, wife of Marcantonio IV Borghese. Florence gave him a worthy welcome. The sumptuous reception was held in the house of the Belle Arti and Grand Duke Ferdinando III of Tuscany was also in attendance. Prince Camillo remarked how impressed he was by the pomp and circumstance that had been arranged to greet him. The grand duke replied that Florence was wont to welcome such noble guests in such a way and asked him to return the hospitality by giving a reception in his own Palazzo Salviati. Camillo had to reply that he did not think his home worthy in its present state for such a sumptuous event. Nevertheless, his pride had been pricked and without prevarication he said that he would hold a reception after he had renovated his palazzo so that it would be fit to welcome a guest like the grand duke, whom he invited for the following Carnival. Ferdinando promised that he would be there,

although he secretly doubted whether it would be possible to complete the renovation in such a short time. This unspoken bet was won by Prince Camillo, who succeeded in renovating the Palazzo Salviati in the Via Ghibellina in just ten months to the plans of the young architect Gaetano Baccani. The reception was held on 31 January 1822, although the grand duke was unable to attend because he was in mourning. But he was invited to another ball, where he marveled at how rapidly and successfully the work had been completed. The previous building, splendid as it was, had in fact been completely rebuilt.

As Mario Bucci wrote, Camillo Borghese was "a person who was untrammeled by any particular traditions or emotional ties to what already existed and was therefore open to total renewal that was completely modern and striking." Baccani in fact followed the wishes of prince Camillo and kept only the loggia and the courtyard of the old building. He exulted in the purest neo-classicism, with a vast, majestic facade, and gold and stucco decorations for the forty halls that were full of

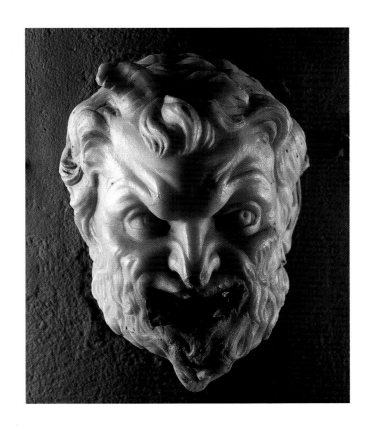

*The entrance hall with its triple loggia and statues of* Venus, *right, and* Diana; *left, the head of a faun in the neo-classical base of the statue of Venus.*

*This page, opposite, and on the following pages, details of the Gallery in all its neo-classical splendor: the framed semicircle of columns, the wide painted ceiling, and, in the following rooms, the gold, the carving, the lights, the stucco work, the period furniture, all reflected in the great mirrors.*

sumptuous furnishings, so that it was said that "Florence was enhanced by a building that was the epitome of elegance."

Nevertheless, the previous Palazzo Salviati had not been bereft of nobility. It was built at the end of the 14th century as a simple house belonging to Iacopo Salviati, between the houses of the Portinari, Donati and Covoni families and the house of the famous Villani family of chroniclers in the area near Bargello, between the Via Ghibellina, Giraldi and Pandolfini. In 1461 Alamanno Salviati extended it by buying the neighboring houses, demolishing them and extending the building to cover a large part of the block, so that it became a palazzo full of columns in a typically 15th-century structure that would stand the test of time and even be incorporated into the rebuilt palazzo.

It was in the early 17th century that Gherardo Silvani renovated the building to give it "the magnificent and grandiose air that we enjoy today," as the art scholar Filippo Baldinucci wrote in 1681 in his appreciation of the triple loggia, which at the time was open, with a background that was enhanced by fine statues of Diana and Apollo. Camillo Borghese instructed Baccani not to destroy the loggia. After it had been enclosed, it became an impressive entrance to the gallery of the *piano nobile*, the *pièce de résistance* of the 1821 renovation, which made the house a social magnet

that the prince had undertaken to create during his meeting with the grand duke. The house was the stage for glittering balls, where, in the words of Mario Bucci, "to the sound of waltzes, gavottes and mazurkas, scandal and indiscretion were exchanged in a rustle of flowing silk gowns."

However, when the seriously sick Pauline Bonaparte arrived in Florence in 1824 to return to her husband Camillo, she did not want to stay in such magnificent surroundings for long. She may have been saddened by the knowledge that she would never enjoy its glory. That winter she moved to Palazzo Strozzi, where she died the following spring. Her husband died in Florence in 1832 and the house passed to his brother Francesco Borghese (1776–1839). He had three children and the palazzo and the noble titles passed to the youngest one, Scipione (1823–98), on condition that he change his surname to Salviati. A Borghese prince thus became a Salviati duke.

Palazzo Salviati was actually sold in 1843 and the new owner, the nobleman Luigi Cappelli, hired out part of it to the Società del Casino di Firenze. This institution was authorized and inaugurated in 1844 by Grand Duke Leopoldo II. The palazzo thus although, only partially, became the haunt of the "cream of Florentine society, who flocked to splendid balls, grandiose competitions and sumptuous banquets." The culminating point of this

*Another richly decorated room where every element of the furnishing has a purity of line that never overwhelms, from the carvings of the doors that evoke the sun gods to the mirror with a gilded and stylized cornice, from the console to the lampstand. Opposite, detail of the door carving*

glory was the period from 1865 to 1870, when Florence was capital of the united Italy. Central to this was the Circolo Borghese, so-called in memory of the man who had created the splendid venue for receptions that became legends, such as the one for the dukes of Austria in 1867 and the one for the princes of Piedmont in 1868.

When the private property of the Tognini Bonelli passed away, the Circolo took over the whole palazzo and to this day it is an emblem of the fashionable spirit in which Prince Camillo Borghese had created it, its social and cultural events recapturing the spirit of former days.

# PALAZZO DEL COMUNE, MONTECATINI TERME

*Right, a decorative detail of the facade.*

*Below, detail of the main facade overlooking the Viale Verdi.*

Although the powers of its healing waters were recognized as long ago as the 15th century, it was only in 1700 that the Lorraine grand duke, Pietro Leopoldo, employing the architect Gaspare Paoletti, created a worthy setting for the "Baths of Montecatini."

As a municipal authority, the small city dates from 1906, when it broke away from the Municipality of Montecatini Val di Nievole, and took its present name in 1928. The Municipality, even before the building of its palazzo, was early on involved in the management of the baths under its first mayor, Egisto Simoncini, who was supported by Pietro Grocco, the government inspector; they were both dedicated to new projects. So in 1913 the architect Ugo Giovagnozzi was invited to Montecatini to give the spa a definite character and improve its health and industrial infrastructure.

The new Montecatini was born at the sign of the *Excelsior*, which was the first avant-garde building in Europe, at once a hotel, a newspaper office, and a theater showing *café chantant* shows. The *Tamerici* and the *Regina*, and the massive *Tettuccio*, were built, and the *Terme Leopoldine* were largely rebuilt, in a radical renovation of the whole town.

"It was the certain 'brilliant future' for the baths of Montecatini that created a pressing need for a municipal building," wrote Carlo Cresti in an article recalling a meeting of the Municipal Council in November 1911 at which great stress was laid on the size the building should be;

*Previous page, top, pictorial decoration by Galileo Chini in the ceiling sprandels and lunettes of the entrance staircase.*

*Right, the sky-light with decoration by Galileo Chini, made by the Fornaci San Lorenzo factory.*

*Bottom right, a detail of the entrance stairway.*

*Previous page, bottom, the staircase and vestibule to the second floor of the palazzo.*

The building of the palace proceeded slowly because of the war, but this turned into an advantage in that it enabled great care to be taken with the inside of the building, which has a magnificent staircase, with a great skylight above, and very extensive pictorial decoration. On the ceiling of the Council Chamber Luigi Arcangeli painted, in a highly rhetorical style, the allegorical figure of *Italia*, a woman with a sword in her hand, dressed in tricolor, and drawn in a chariot by two black horses towards Victory. In the ceiling lunettes and pendentives, Galileo Chini painted a series of allegorical figures representing *Peace*, *Victory*, *Knowledge*, and *Labor*. The Palazzo Comunale reflects the spa-town atmosphere with which Montecatini is synonymous, and which celebrates not only well-being and health, but the fashionable world of all the famous personalities, both Italian and foreign, who over the years have honored this city: sovereigns, musicians, painters, poets.

*Left, pictorial decoration on the ceiling of the Municipal Council Room, representing* The Apotheosis of Italy, *by Luigi Arcangeli.*

*The monumental entrance stairway of the Palazzo del Comunale.*

"a palazzo both large and modern" that would symbolize the ambitions of the municipality and "add to the summer attraction of our countryside, which in itself has something of art about it." At first it was intended to launch a national competition, but it was then felt that "this would lead to a serious loss of time." Consequently, the decision was cancelled, and the design was entrusted to the Montecatini architect Raffaello Brizzi, on the understanding that the palazzo would be "attractive, modern, magnificent, artistic, and practical." But this was not all, because, in order that there should be some municipal control of the building of the palazzo, Brizzi was joined by the engineer Luigi Righetti.

The plan was eventually drawn up in 1913: a building modeled on 16th-century Florentine palaces, with all the magnificence required and with elements described by Carlo Cresti as "the long balcony of the main facade supported by projecting columns, the steps and entrance ramps that give vitality to the lower part of the building, the cornice strongly marked out by the relief of the trusses, the sequence of coupled columns that on the fourth floor characterize the central section of the facade looking on to the Viale Verdi."

# Tuscany from the High Middle Ages to Italian Unification

by Ludger Scherer

In the first millennium BC what is today Tuscany was inhabited by the Etruscans, a people who were later conquered and absorbed by the Romans. The Roman word "tusci" was the origin of the name *Tuscia* for Central Italy, but since the Middle Ages the region has been known as Tuscany ("Toscana" in Italian).

As far back as the Etruscan era, Tuscany's cities played a dominant role in shaping the region's cultural landscape; individual city states attempted to gain control over the surrounding countryside in order to exploit it for agriculture. Several of the towns that would later become fierce rivals - such as Arezzo, Volterra and Fiesole - are of Etruscan origin while others - like Pisa, Lucca, Pistoia and Florence - were Roman colonies. After the collapse of the western Roman Empire in 476 AD the area went into decline and the achievements of its civilisation, such as the urban architecture and the network of Roman roads, crumbled away. Like the rest of the country, Tuscany fell under the sway of a succession of foreign overlords: Ostrogoths, Langobards and Franks. During the reign of the Langobards (568-774) the royal capitals of Lucca and Pisa dominated the former Roman regional capital of Florence, a state of affairs which would not be reversed until several centuries later.

Feudal structures were broadened under the Carolingians and these gave rise to the margravate of Tuszien which expanded in size and power under the margravine Mathilde. No loyal supporter of the Emperor, Mathilde supported the cities in their efforts to gain autonomy; when she died childless in 1115, she left her estates to the Holy See in her will, thus intensifying the conflict between the emperor and the pope in Tuscany. In the High Middle Ages, the centuries-old battle over the secular power and property of the church took the form of an investiture dispute concerning the appointment of bishops. When an agreement was finally reached at the Concord of Worms in 1122, the Empire was left in a considerably weakened position. The cities and communities of upper and central Italy used this enduring conflict to consolidate their own power and expand their territories.

Although their nominal sovereignty was never disputed, the emperors of the Hohenstaufen dynasty were never able to forcibly reintroduce feudal structures when opposed by the powerful city states. Depending on the nature of their interests at the time, the cities would ally themselves with either the Imperial or Papal party: their one unwavering concern was always to gain the upper hand over the neighboring town.

From the eleventh century, Pisa, which had access to the sea, noticeably strengthened its economic position with respect to Lucca, Pistoia, Florence and Siena. Merchants were able to develop trading connections as far as Flanders, especially in the cloth trade, and they became the financial backers of popes, emperors and kings. Administrative reforms also became necessary in the rapidly growing cities, causing city councils to appoint a so-called *podestà*, a mayor, who was provided with executive powers for a limited term.

In the twelfth century the cities attempted to extend their power base into the surrounding countryside (*contado*) and were opposed by the feudal nobility. The aim of this move was to dominate an entire diocese from a single city. Due to their proximity, the two bishoprics of Florence and Fiesole competed fiercely, and in 1125 this led to the conquest and destruction of Fiesole. The territorial policies of the larger cities, as the case of Florence clearly shows, were conducted with considerable aggression. In order to secure their political and economic power, rival cities entered into alliances which were generally dictated by the logic of geography: Siena was allied with Pisa against Florence which was supported by Lucca and San Gimignano. These divisions were complicated by the conflict already discussed between the pope and emperor and at the beginning of the thirteenth century, which led to the factions of the Guelfs and Ghibellines being formed. (The names were derived from the supporters of Emperor Frederick II from Waiblingen - *ghibellino* - and those of the pope and his favorite Otto IV, the Guelf, or *guelfo*.) While Florence and Lucca pursued pro-Guelf policies in the hope of achieving advantages in international trade and avoiding demands for Imperial tribute, the Ghibelline cities of Siena and Pisa supported the emperor in order to fend off the powerful Florentines. The Guelfs later split into a black and a white, or moderate, faction. Dante was a member of the Bianchi (Whites) and after the victory of the Neri (Blacks) in 1302 he was exiled from Florence for life. After the death of Frederick II in 1250 yet another power appeared on the scene in the form of Charles of Anjou, the brother of the French king. Originally called by the Pope to assist him in his struggles with the last of the Hohenstaufen in Lower Italy, the House of Anjou proceeded to extend its domains to Northern Italy in the thirteenth and fourteenth centuries through an alliance with the Guelf cities.

Up until the fifteenth century few of the city republics emerged as victors in the military conflicts described here: Lucca achieved some success, as did Siena, which extended its sway over Montepulciano (1249), Massa Marittima (1335), Grosseto (1336) and Chiusi (1416) but both these towns were outstripped by Florence, which gained control over Pistoia (1329), Prato (1351), San Gimignano (1354), Volterra (1361), Cortona (1411) as well as Pisa (1406).

The economic and political upturn, however, was hampered in the fourteenth century by the plague, famine and the insolvency of the great banking houses. During this period the *popolo*, the people, seized power in several cities for the first time though this meant the wealthy citizenry (*popolo grasso*) rather than the poor (*popolo minuto*). Other cities responded to the difficulties of the age with increasingly oligarchic structures. Powerful guilds claimed the exclusive right to rule and in 1293 the Florentine constitution guaranteed them sole access to public office. The office of the Gonfaloniere was set up as the chief executive body; and a council of the Priori (heads of the guilds) formed the Signoria (city council). Republican institutions were retained, at least nominally, and it was not until the rise of the Medici that a single family was able to gain control of the city and, later, the entire region.

The Medici family began to build up their power base after the abortive rising of the Ciompi (woollen workers) in 1378; and in 1434 Cosimo il Vecchio (the Elder) de' Medici (1398–1464) finally became effective ruler of Florence. The diplomatic skills and cautious policies of the Medici meant that a long period of peace was now ushered in. Under Piero il Gottoso (the Gouty) (1416–1469) and Lorenzo il Magnifico (the Magnificent) (1449–1492) culture flourished in Florence. In April 1478 Lorenzo survived an assassination attempt in the cathedral which however cost the life of his brother Giuliano: a conspiracy by the Pazzi, a rival family, had failed to achieve its goal.

Medici rule was interrupted in 1494 when the family was expelled and the republic restored after the French king, Charles VIII, invaded Italy. The fanatical Dominican monk, Girolamo Savonarola, renowned for his impassioned sermons and apocalyptic prophecies, reorganised the city into a theocracy. The experiment was short-lived, however; Savonarola was executed in 1498 and though the Republic lingered on it was ultimately reconquered for the Medici in 1512.

While the French monarchs, the popes and the Habsburgs under Charles V all struggled for supremacy in Italy, Cosimo I, as head of the Medici family, was able to extend his new duchy of Tuscany by defeating and incorporating Siena (1559). In 1570 he was crowned Grand Duke by the pope.

The seventeenth century saw the Medicis' glory go into terminal decline, and when the last of their rulers died without issue in 1737, the Grand Duchy passed to Franz Stephan of Lorraine. Under his son Peter Leopold (1765–1792) Tuscany developed into the very model of a modern state; he reorganized commerce, the administration and agriculture in the spirit of enlightened Absolutism. With the exception of the Napoleonic era from 1799–1814 the Hapsburgs ruled the Grand Duchy until 1859. Napoleon Bonaparte campaigned in Italy against the Austrians from 1796, establishing the Cisalpine Republic, later the Kingdom of Italy, in the north of the country. In 1802 the Hapsburgs lost their grip on Tuscany when it became part of the Kingdom of Etruria under the House of Bourbon-Parma, but in 1808 it was annexed by France.

The restoration of the old order arranged at the Congress of Vienna (1814/15) was only briefly able to halt the formation of nation-states; in Italy the socio-political movement of the *Risorgimento* paved the way for the country's unification. Giuseppe Mazzini and his group *Giovine Italia* (Young Italy) represented the revolutionary-republican wing though they were unable to get their demands accepted because of opposition from moderate reformers around the Piedmontese politician Camillo Benso di Cavour. The Austrians were driven out of the country in 1859 with French help and the Italian regions – including the southern Italian territories conquered by Garibaldi – were annexed to the Kingdom of Piedmont. In 1861 Vittorio Emanuele of Piedmont became King of Italy. For six years from 1864 Florence was capital city of the kingdom until the Roman Question was temporarily resolved in 1871 through the incorporation of the Vatican City into Italy.

# BIBLIOGRAPHY

ACKERMAN, J.S., *The Architecture of Michelangelo*, London 1961.

ACTON, H., *Tuscan Villas*, London 1973.

ACTON, H., *The Last Medici*, rev. edn, London 1958; illustr. edn, 1980.

ACTON, H. & E. CHANEY, *Florence: A Travellers' Companion*, London 1986.

ADY, C. M., *Lorenzo de' Medici and Renaissance Italy*, London 1955.

AMMIRATO S., *Istorie fiorentine*, Firenze 1824–27.

ARGAN, G., *The Renaissance City*, New York 1969.

BARACCHINI C. (a cura di), *Pisa dei Cavalieri*, Milano 1996.

BARON, H., *The Crisis of the Early Italian Renaissance*, rev. edn, Princeton 1966.

BELLI BARSALI I., *Lucca. Guida alla città*, Lucca 1988.

BELLI BARSALI I. (a cura di), *I palazzi dei mercanti nella libera Lucca del '500. Immagine di una città-stato al tempo dei Medici*, catalogo della mostra, Lucca 1980.

BERENSON, B., *Italian Painters of the Renaissance*, London 1930.

BIGAZZI I., *Il palazzo Nonfinito*, Bologna 1977.

BORSI F., *Firenze nel Cinquecento*, Roma 1974.

BORSOOK, E., *Ambrogio Lorenzetti*, Florenz 1966.

BORTONE S., *Guida alla civiltà di Firenze*, Milano 1985.

BRANDI C. (a cura di), *Il Palazzo Pubblico di Siena, Vicende costruttive e decorazioni*, Milano 1983.

BRUCKER, G.A., *Renaissance Florence*, Berkeley, Calif. 1969.

BRUCKER, G.A.(ed.), *The Civic World of Early Renaissance Florence*, Princeton 1977.

BUCCI M., BENCINI R., *Palazzi di Firenze (4 voll.)*, Firenze 1971–1973.

BUONARROTI M., *Le rime e le lettere*, Milano 1927.

BURKE, P., *Culture and Society in Renaissance Italy*, London 1972.

CABANI R., *Le famiglie di Firenze (4 voll.)*, Firenze 1992.

CAIROLA A., CARLI E., *Il palazzo Pubblico di Siena*, Roma 1963.

CAMBI G., *Istorie*, Firenze 1785–86.

CARDINI F., RAVEGGI S., *Palazzi pubblici di Toscana. I centri minori*, Firenze 1983.

CARLI, E., *Volterra nel Medioevo e nel Rinascimento*, Pisa 1978.

CARLI, E. & G. CECCHINI, *San Gimignano*, Milano 1962.

CASOTTI G.B., *Diario, Biblioteca Riccardiana*, cod. 1184.

CHERUBINI G., FANELLI G. (a cura di), *Il palazzo Medici Riccardi di Firenze*, Firenze 1990.

CIVAI M., TOTI E., *Siena. Il sogno gotico*, Siena 1997.

CLEUGH, J., *The Medici*, London 1989.

COCHRANE, E., *Florence in the Forgotten Centuries 1527–1800*, Chicago 1973.

CONTI C., *Il Palazzo Pitti, la sua primitiva costruzione e i successivi ingrandimenti*, Firenze 1887.

CRESTI C., *Montecatini 1771–1940: nascita e sviluppo di una città termale*, Milano 1984.

CRESTI C., NANNONI D., *Architettura senza cantiere. Immagini architettoniche nella pittura e scultura del Rinascimento*, Siena 1989.

DE' MEDICI L., *Ricordi*, London 1847.

FABBRI, P. & F. Gurrieri, *Palaces of Florence*, Florence 1996.

FIUMI E., *Volterra e San Gimignano nel Medioevo*, San Gimignano 1983.

GAGE, J., *Life in Italy at the Time of the Medici*, London 1968.

GANDI G., *Il palazzo Ramirez di Montalvo*, Firenze 1932.

GIAMPAOLI U., *Il Palazzo Ducale di Massa*, Massa 1986.

GINORI LISCI, L., *The Palazzi of Florence: Their History and Art, 2 vols.*, Florence 1985.

GIULIETTI R., *La Quadreria del Palazzo Comunale di Monte San Savino*, Monte San Savino 1997.

GODFREY, F.M., *Italian Architecture up to 1750*, London 1971.

GOLDTHWAITE, R. A., *The Building of Renaissance Florence*, Baltimore/London 1980.

GOLDTHWAITE, R. A., *The Florentine Palace as Domestic Architecture*, American Historical Review, 1972.

GRIFONI P., DALLA NEGRA R., *I palazzi Tarugi e Sinatti sulla piazza Grande di Montepulciano, in "Quaderni dell'Istituto di Storia dell'Architettura"*, Università di Roma, 1982, fasc. 169–174.

GUICCIARDINI F., *Opere*, Milano 1961.

GUICCIARDINI P., DORI E., *Le antiche case e il palazzo dei Guicciardini in Firenze*, Firenze 1951.

HALE, J.R., *Florence and the Medici: The Pattern of Control*, London 1977.

HERLIHY, D., *Pisa in the early Renaissance. A study of urban growth*, New Haven 1958.

HIBBERT, C., *The Rise and Fall of the House of Medici*, London 1974.

HIBBERT, C., *Florence: The Biography of a City*, London 1993.

JAMES, H., *Italian Hours*, London 1909.

KARWACKA CODINI E., *Piazza dei Cavalieri a Pisa*, Firenze 1989.

KAUFFMAN, G., *Florence: Art Treasures and Buildings*, London 1971.

KENT, F. W., *Household and Lineage in Renaissance Florence: The Family Life of the Capponi, Ginori and Rucellai*, Princeton 1977.

KENT, F. W., *"Più superbo de quella de Lorenzo": Courtly & Family Interest in the Building of Filippo Strozzis Palace*, in: Renaissance Quarterly 30, 1977.

LANDUCCI, L., *Diario*, London 1927.

LENSI A., *Il palazzo degli Antinori*, Firenze 1939.

LISTRI F., *Il Dizionario di Firenze (2 vol.)*, Firenze 1998–99.

LUSINI V., *Storia del palazzo Chigi Saracini*, I, Siena 1927.

MACK, C. R., *Pienza. The creation of a Renaissance City*, Italica/London 1987.

MANDELLI E., *Palazzi del Rinascimento*, Firenze 1989.

MANSI G., *Il palazzo dei Mansi a San Pellegrino*, Lucca s.d.

MANSI G., *I patrizi di Lucca*, Lucca 1996.

MARCHINI G., Giuliano da Sangallo, Firenze 1943.

MARTINES, L., *Violence and Disorder in Italian Cities*, Berkeley, Calif. 1972.

MARTINI G.C., *Viaggio in Toscana (1725–1745)*, Modena 1969.

MASSINELLI, A. M. & F. TUENA, *Treasures of the Medici*, London 1992.

MCCARTHY, M., *The Stones of Florence*, New York 1959.

MEISS, M., *Painting in Florence and Siena after the Black Death in the Mid-Fourteenth Century*, New York 1951.

MERCANTINI M., *Il palazzo di Fraternita in piazza Grande ad Arezzo*, Arezzo 1980.

MILLON, H.A. & V. Magnago Lampugnani (ed.), *The Renaissance from Brunelleschi to Michelangelo. The Representation of Architecture*, London 1994.

MINOR, A.C. & B. MITCHELL, *A Renaissance Entertainment: Festivities for the Marriage of Cosimo I*, University of Missouri Press, 1968.

MORISANI O., *Michelozzo architetto*, Torino 1951.

MOSCATO A., *Il palazzo Pazzi a Firenze*, Roma 1963.

MUCCINI U., *Il salone dei Cinquecento in palazzo Vecchio*, Firenze 1990.

MUCCINI U., CECCHI A., *Le stanze del Principe in Palazzo Vecchio*, Firenze 1992.

MURRAY, P., *The Architecture of the Italian Renaissance*, London 1969.

NARDI J., *Istorie della città di Firenze*, Torino 1852.

PAMPALONI G., *Palazzo Strozzi*, Roma 1982.

PAOLUCCI A., MAETZKE A.M., *La Casa del Vasari in Arezzo*, Firenze 1988.

PAZZAGLI C., *Nobiltà civile e sangue blu*, Firenze 1996.

PELLEGRINI E., *Palazzi e vie di Siena nelle opere a stampa dal XVI al XX secolo*, Siena 1987.

PICCOLOMINI, Enea Silvio, *Memoirs of a Renaissance Pope: The Commentaries of Pius II*, 1959.

POGGI G., *Or San Michele*, Firenze 1895.

POPE-HENNESSY, J., *Italian High Renaissance and Baroque Sculpture*, rev. edn, London 1970.

POTTINGER, G., *The Court of the Medici*, London 1978.

RAGIONIERI P., *Casa Buonarroti*, Firenze 1997.

RODOLICO N., MARCHINI G., *I palazzi del popolo nei comuni toscani del Medioevo*, Milano 1962.

ROMBY G.C. (a cura di), *Misure e proporzioni dell'architettura nel tardo Quattrocento. Materiali da costruzione e misure nell'edilizia fiorentina*, Firenze 1996.

ROSS J., *Florentine Palaces and their Stories*, London 1905.

ROWLEY, G., *Ambrogio Lorenzetti*, Princeton UP 1958.

RUBINSTEIN N., *Palazzi pubblici e palazzi privati al tempo di Brunelleschi*, in AA.VV., *Filippo Brunelleschi. La sua opera e il suo tempo*, Firenze 1980.

RUD, E., *Vasari's Life and Lives*, London 1964.

RUGGIERI F., *Studio d'architettura civile sopra le fabbriche insigni di Firenze*, Firenze 1722–1755.

SAALMAN H., *Il palazzo comunale di Montepulciano, un lavoro sconosciuto di Michelozzo*, Siena 1973.

SALMI M., *Il palazzo e la collezione Chigi Saracini*, Milano 1967.

SANPAOLESI P., *Il palazzo Pitti e gli architetti fiorentini della discendenza brunelleschiana*, in "Scritti vari di storia, restauro e critica dell'architettura", Firenze 1978.

STRONG, R., *Splendour at Court: Renaissance Spectacle and Illusion*, London 1973.

THIEM G. e C., *Toskanische Fassadendekoration in Sgrafito und Fresko*, München 1964.

TRIONFI HONORATI M., *Il palazzo degli Antinori*, in "Antichità Viva", 1968.

VANNUCCI M., *Splendidi palazzi di Firenze*, Firenze 1995.

VASARI, Giorgio, *Lives of the Artists*, Harmondsworth 1965.

WALEY, D., *Italian City Republics*, London 1988.

AA.VV., *Raffaello e l'architettura a Firenze nella prima metà del Cinquecento*, Firenze 1984.

AA.VV., *La sede storica del Monte dei Paschi di Siena. Vicende costruttive e opere d'arte*, Siena 1988.

AA.VV., *Il palazzo Medici-Riccardi a Firenze*, Firenze 1990.

AA.VV., *Il tempo di Alberico 1553–1623. Alberico I Cybo-Malaspina signore, politico e mecenate a Massa e a Carrara, catalogo della mostra*, Pisa 1991.

AA.VV., *Bartolomeo Ammannati. Scultore e architetto 1511–1592*, Firenze 1995.

AA.VV., *La casa del Cancelliere. Documenti e studi sul palazzo di Bartolomeo Scala a Firenze*, Firenze 1998.

# INDEX

317

*Photograph credits*

All the photographs are by Massimo Listri, with the following exceptions:

SCALA PHOTOGRAPHIC ARCHIVE: pp. 11 top, 19, 21, 22, 23, 29, 47 top, 178.

MAGNUS ARCHIVE: pp. 34 bottom left, 35, 49, 70-71 top, 79, 86 right, 90, 98 top, 102 top, 177, 181.

BENCINI PHOTOGRAPHIC ARCHIVE: pp. 42-43, 88 top, 91, 93, 94, 96-97, 98 bottom, 99 bottom, 100, 101, 102 bottom, 103, 104.

QUATTRONE PHOTOGRAPHIC ARCHIVE: pp. 66, 70 bottom, 72 right, 99 top, 105 right, 180.

FMR PHOTOGRAPHIC ARCHIVE: pp. 179 top, 290, 291.

SIME PHOTOGRAPHIC ARCHIVE: pp. 62-63.

THE DRAWINGS & PRINTS DEPARTMENT OF THE UFFIZI: p. 47 bottom.

CIOL PHOTOGRAPHIC ARCHIVE: p. 86 left.

SCALETTI PHOTOGRAPHIC ARCHIVE: p. 307 top.